The
Product
Liability
Mess

How Business
Can Be Rescued
from the Politics
of State Courts

RICHARD NEELY

THE FREE PRESS
A Division of Macmillan, Inc.
NEW YORK

Collier Macmillan Publishers
LONDON

The Free Press
A Division of Macmillan, Inc.
866 Third Avenue, New York, N.Y. 10022

Collier Macmillan Canada, Inc.

Printed in the United States of America

printing number
1 2 3 4 5 6 7 8 9 10

Library of Congress Cataloging-in-Publication Data

Neely, Richard
    The product liability mess.

    Bibliography: p.
    Includes index.
    1. Products liability—United States.   2. Insurance,
Products liability—United States.   3. Damages—United
States.   4. Corporations, Foreign—United States—States.
5. Courts—United States—States.   6. United States.
Supreme Court.   I. Title.
KF1296.N44   1988   346.7303′82   87–33196
ISBN 0–02–922680–5   347.306382

For my son, John, who always helps me lay the fire on winter weekends as I settle down to write.

Nowhere has the philosophical argument been evaded, but where it runs out into too thin a thread the Author has preferred to cut it short, and fall back upon the corresponding results of experience; for in the same way as many plants only bear fruit when they do not shoot too high, so in the practical arts the theoretical leaves and flowers must not be made to sprout too far, but kept near to experience, which is their proper soil.

—Karl von Clausewitz, *On War*

Contents

Acknowledgments

In the course of writing this book, I have had the help of many people. My preeminent thanks go to the members of my own staff, particularly my administrative assistant, Betty Barnsgrove Price. Betty generally supervised the preparation of the manuscript, typed and retyped the chapters, and also read everything carefully to ensure that what was written was intelligible to an interested lay-person. Special thanks are also in order to my secretary, Lea Ann Litton, who typed late into the night to get my manuscript out on time. My brilliant law clerk, Barry Cushman, worked with me on the substance and language of the manuscript and mobilized his friends and associates around the country to check the accuracy of our observations.

My editor, Grant Ujifusa, made valuable contributions to the concept, wording, structure, and even the content of the book. And, of course, I would not be in the writing business at all were it not for the eleemosynary undertakings of my agent, Marian Young of the Young Agency, who believes that what I do may, on occasion, be valuable, although it loses her money! Finally, I am grateful to my friend, Professor Cecil Y. Lang of the University of Virginia, who did his usual excellent editing job to ensure that many lawyerisms were eliminated, and that my usage and grammar were up to acceptable standards of literacy (for a lawyer).

Fairmont, West Virginia

August 2, 1987

Introduction

Larry Tribe and Richard Epstein, two leading constitutional theorists, can't write this book. The reason is that both are brilliant lawyers, while I am an ordinary state judge and politician. The fact is, however, that too much brilliance, and too nice a regard for the intricacies of legal theories, can affect a person's appreciation of how to deliver a bold blow to the political jugular. Today's problems of liability in general, and of product liability in particular, require new political strategies and not new legal theories. As John Kennedy discovered early in his career, the view of the world from a barstool in Charlestown is very different from what is seen from an office at the Harvard Law School. Most of the voters live in Charlestown and not in Harvard Square.

Unlike others who have written about America's liability crisis, I am not a neutral, scholarly, outside observer. In fact, up to this very moment in my life I have been part of the problem rather than part of the solution. As a state court judge, much of my time is devoted to designing elaborate new ways to make business pay for everyone else's bad luck. I may not always congratulate myself at the end of the day on the brilliance of my legal reasoning, but when I do such things as allow a paraplegic to collect a few hundred thousand dollars from the Michelin Tire Company—thanks to a one-car crash of unexplainable cause—I at least sleep well at night. Michelin will somehow survive (and if they don't, only the French will care), but my disabled constituent won't make it the rest of her life without Michelin's money.

In the entire area of liability, the real problem for American society is that my microproblem as a judge who wants to sleep at

1

night has begun to create a macroproblem for the entire economy. The man on the barstool in Charlestown, however, is not interested in speculative macroproblems that do not yet intrude into his everyday life. Macroproblems become real to him only when he, his family, or his friends lose their jobs or can't find a doctor. Right now liability law helps the man on the barstool and everyone dear to him: liability law is a massive, off-line, wealth-redistribution program that enjoys overwhelming popular support. Yet many of us who administer the liability law are coming to understand that the macroproblem exists, and that something should be done about it before its unhappy consequences become all too apparent to the man on the barstool.

If, however, we were to try to enlist the support of the man on the barstool to do something about the impending liability crisis, he would be profoundly uncooperative. For him, liability law hasn't closed any big companies, nor has it ruined his family's level of medical care. All that he can see today is that when working people get hurt they can get some money from the fat cats, and now doctors make less money and are forced to be more careful. Furthermore, the pervasive worldview among barstool sitters does not appear to be contradicted by expert studies. Indeed, some companies have been put out of business by the rising cost of liability insurance, and other companies have been bankrupted by product liability judgments, but these are not common occurrences capable of arousing concern in the average voter. Certainly no tears have been shed by anyone for A. H. Robins or Johns Manville, who have inflicted severe injuries on the public in the pursuit of private profit.

But if there is not convincing evidence that the *current* liability system will do very bad things to the American economy, there is increasing evidence that the logical extension of our current liability system will do very bad things indeed. And, if any one thing is certain, it is that the off-line, wealth-redistribution system will be extended more and more, as long as state court judges want to sleep well at night and help their neighbors and constituents. In 1987, for example, in the two Florida counties around Miami, malpractice insurance jumped 47 percent in one year and caused a doctors' strike. Increases in liability costs of this magnitude cannot continue indefinitely without serious consequences for both the price and availability of health care.

Data supporting the conclusion that liability law is going to become a progressively more prominent hazard for the economy is all around us. Unfortunately, all science, and particularly the science of law, is a social undertaking. Scientific theories are intellectual constructs that we impose upon data; they are not intellectual constructs that are demanded by the data. When people have political reasons for not wanting to believe a particular theory, they simply reorganize the data to support another, politically more palatable theory. One such politically palatable theory about the liability crisis is that insurance companies are behind the crisis, driven by insatiable greed. But careful review of the profit-and-loss figures does not bear this out, if we give due consideration to the need for reserves and the dramatic reduction in interest rates that occurred between 1981 and 1986. Nonetheless, the insurance companies are sufficiently greedy and sufficiently arrogant that they lend credence to the greed theory. The man on the barstool is convinced that we will be able to handle everything just the way it is once the insurance companies are forced to be fair; he is also convinced that there is enough money somewhere to go around.

When experienced lawyers try to tackle our liability problem they usually just conclude that we are at an impasse, given the balance of countervailing political forces. Accordingly, the best they can do is suggest new, narrower liability rules for adoption by our fifty state court systems. This suggestion, however, is like admonishing alcoholics not to drink. So the modest virtue of my book is that I am willing to say (metaphorically, of course), "I am an alcoholic and I need help."

What is needed to fend off the impending liability crisis is a battle plan for a successful guerrilla campaign that will bypass entirely the intensely fortified political positions of a numerically and logistically superior opposing force. Twenty years ago I was an army captain in Vietnam; there I learned that when outnumbered and outgunned peasants take on standing armies head to head, they lose badly. But I also learned that a standing army has little defense against a good guerrilla force, backed by a competent propaganda campaign. The basic political problem that we currently have in reforming liability law is that the reformers are convinced they must play by the enemy's rules. But if we change the rules we can change the war, and that's the only way reformers can win.

Recent books about the liability crisis have succeeded only in describing the evolution and operation of the present legal system and the problems that the system creates. When it comes to a blueprint for action, academic commentators either throw up their hands or propose solutions that are no more practical than yet another editorial in the *Wall Street Journal*. Neither failure, however, is particularly blameworthy: the lack of politically feasible remedies simply lends credence to the old Chinese observation that the existence of a problem does not necessarily imply the existence of a solution. And, as the man on the barstool instinctively understands, the solution that emerges from the minds of the pointy-headed elite who are employed by corporate giants, and who never worry about being disabled from doing manual labor, is frequently worse than the problem.

The basic problem with liability law is not that lawyers and judges lack the imagination to invent new, fairer rules that will avert the coming crisis. The problem is entirely political: the logic of collective action implies that no one state or group of states will undertake to act responsibly to curtail off-line wealth redistribution, given irresponsibility on the part of neighboring states. Obviously, it is not possible to create an entirely risk-free society; therefore, today's big question for the law professors is where collective responsibility for accidents ends and individual responsibility begins. I do not know where we should draw that line; even if I were smart enough to figure it out, the practical importance of my labor would not amount to much.

The anarchy that currently prevails among American state jurisdictions absolutely guarantees *politically* that no line of any sort will ever be drawn. After all, I'm not the only appellate judge in America who wants to sleep at night. As long as I am allowed to redistribute wealth from out-of-state companies to injured in-state plaintiffs, I shall continue to do so. Not only is my sleep enhanced when I give someone else's money away, but so is my job security, because the in-state plaintiffs, their families, and their friends will reelect me.

Drawing a line around business's tort liability, then, must inevitably be done at the national level. Currently there are bills before Congress that attempt to limit different types of tort liability, particularly product liability, yet the chances of their passing in any form, much less a form favorable to business, are exceedingly small. This is because the man on the barstool is mostly interested in money today, and not in what's going to happen to the economy at some hypothetical, macrolevel tomorrow. Ironically, then, the most likely place for new "legislation" controlling liability to be adopted is the Supreme Court of the United States.

Business executives tend to identify with the conservative side in American politics, and in conservative political circles "states' rights" are taken as a matter of faith. Realistically, of course, a knee-jerk states' rights position simply works backwards from the political results desired—lower taxes, less government intrusion, fewer "liberal" solutions to social problems, and stronger traditional institutions—to a general theory that more often than not leads to such results. Thus, a non-specialized business audience would immediately find unpalatable a suggestion that more stringent regulation of the state courts by the U.S. Supreme Court would be good for business.

Indeed, it is the counter-intuitive nature of the proposed court-imposed solution to the liability problem here that makes it so politically feasible. Dean Rusk once told me that, after Earl Warren's retirement from the U.S. Supreme Court, Justice Warren went to speak at the University of Georgia, where Secretary Rusk was teaching, and told a small group of law professors that the primary political function of the courts was to break the impasses that are inherent in any structure of balanced powers. Business generally regards such power to break impasses as working to its detriment, because of the anti-business Supreme Court decisions that have followed the Court's recent "liberal," equal-rights agenda. But the perception of intractable court hostility to business is incorrect if we look at the relationship between the court and business over the last hundred years. It is the very ability to break structural impasses that renders the U.S. Supreme Court the potential prime mover in product liability reform.

Historically, business has fared very well at the hands of the U.S. Supreme Court. The courts have always been interested in the vibrancy of the American economy, and the earliest occasions for judicial activism in the United States were intrusions into the political process (the breaking of impasses) *on behalf of* business. In this regard the Supreme Court both created and then steadfastly defended the American free-trade zone by eliminating almost all state-imposed barriers to interstate commerce. As recently as June 1987, in two cases coming from California, the U.S. Supreme Court held that if state or local government overregulates land use, the regulating government must condemn the land. The existing local government exposure as a result of these two decisions alone is conservatively estimated by experts at over a trillion dollars! As a direct result of the Court's ruling, the mayor of San Francisco immediately vetoed three new zoning ordinances passed by the city council. Indeed, it is difficult to imagine a more dramatic pro-business result than the two taking cases, yet they were concurred in or even written by the Court's most "liberal" members.

Accordingly, I ask the business reader to engage in the willing suspension of disbelief for at least four or five chapters while I place the courts in proper perspective as political, policymaking institutions, and while I make the case that many of the apparently irrational results in liability law that we get from the courts today come from a structural problem in the design of America's chaotic court system, rather than from any intentional, anti-business bias. Furthermore, if the book is not slammed shut too quickly, the reader should come to see that the federal courts have available to them all of the tools necessary to make a big dent in the liability problem, and even to do it in such a way that not only will business be better off, but also the victims of accidents. The startling result that both plaintiffs and defendants can be made better off at the same time comes from the fact that much motion and money are currently lost litigating matters that could be quickly and cheaply settled if we had firm, understandable, bright-line rules.

Furthermore, as I shall demonstrate later, the model for a new national common law of liability in general, and of product liability in particular, has been successfully tried twice in the last twenty-five years—once in the unification of state criminal law, and again in the elimination of most liability for the media under state libel and slander law. Therefore, all of the technology necessary to reform helter-skelter liability law is already in place, and it is now simply a matter of getting the issue of certain types of liability, particularly product liability, on the national judicial agenda.

Consequently, my emphasis in this book is not on technical legal arguments, but rather on exploring the social structures from which the current liability law emerges. The reason is that the foundation of all law is social structure. For example, I am a back-woods judge who decides ordinary cases that are of absolutely no concern to anyone but the litigants. Most of my day is consumed by working as the inside man at the judicial skunkworks where I slog through tedious criminal, workers' compensation, and product liability cases. If I say to myself, "the hell with those Frenchmen at Michelin!" and give some injured West Virginian a few hundred thousand dollars, it doesn't shatter the foundations of West Virginia's commercial world. Since I'm paid to choose between deciding for Michelin and sleeping well, I choose sleeping well. Why hurt my friends when there's no percentage in it?

But the justices of the Supreme Court of the United States are not real judges like me. Supreme Court justices are legislators who control a large percentage of all of our law through their decisions interpreting the Constitution or federal statutes. While, as a state judge, deciding against Michelin helps me sleep, if I were on the U.S. Supreme Court and did the same things that I do now I would not ever sleep. The reason is simple: when you decide any case on the U.S. Supreme Court you are making law that will govern the entire country for a long time. Consequently, you had better be right! Any Supreme Court decision is telegraphed within minutes to every part of the United States, where it is immediately generalized to control any ongoing issue that is even vaguely similar to the case that was decided. If the U.S. Supreme Court takes over the rules governing liability in America, they must be constantly mindful that they are tinkering at the superstructure of the whole American economy.

Unfortunately, the action required by business to reform liability law is substantially more complicated than simply voting a straight Republican ticket, or sending money to a hardworking PAC. Indeed, getting the product liability problem on the agenda of the U.S. Supreme Court will require some significant political spadework, but this book should provide the preliminary blueprint. Here it is important to remember that three justices of the U.S. Supreme Court are now about eighty, and the next administration is likely to appoint as many as four new justices. The civil rights and civil liberties agenda that has engaged the U.S. Supreme Court for the last twenty-five years has about played itself out: the great strides that can be made in those areas by the judiciary have already been made, and now all that is required is preventive maintenance on an existing judicial machine. Yet no high-ranking political official, such as a Supreme Court justice, wants to be an unimaginative epigone: tomorrow's new Supreme Court justices will be in search of a new agenda. I would like to provide at least part of that agenda.

Chapter 1

Business and the Courts

Product liability law began to assume its current outline about twenty-five years ago. Since that time it has evolved into an increasingly prominent hazard for American business; each new adjustment in the law only makes it more difficult to defend product liability suits. By the mid-1970's business had made the reform of product liability law a priority item on its political agenda, yet business has had no success, at either the federal or state levels, in rolling back the product liability juggernaut. Notwithstanding massive campaign contributions to congressmen and senators (and many outright bribes in the form of speaking honoraria), business thus far has failed to persuade Congress to undertake any substantial reform of our nation's tort system; nor is business going to do any better in Congress in the future.

Product liability law, along with most other tort law, is a creation of the courts. For reasons that I shall explore in more detail later, it is eminently unlikely that Congress will tinker at the massive wealth-redistribution program that is already in place. Tort "reform" in any guise has about as much chance of getting through Congress as social security "reform." Regardless of its unwholesome effects on employment, investment, operating costs, and profits, product liability law has made the United States the safest country in the world. As a result, not even businessmen are in favor of dismantling the entire product liability system. Strangely enough, however, the institution that brought us product liability law in the first place—namely, the courts—is the institution most likely to change product liability law to make it more rational and less costly. The reason is simple: the courts now have almost exclusive control over the product liability system, and that system is getting out of hand.

Over the last thirty years there has been a wholesale shift in the center of political power in the United States in the direction of the courts. As a result, courts today are a prominent political hazard for the majority of America's businesses. But courts are like any other high-class political institution: they are legitimately interested in making the country prosperous, efficient, and humane. Courts are not out to beat up on business as a matter of principle, and, in areas other than product liability, courts are often the best friend business has in the political process. Certainly business frequently prefers the decisions it gets from the courts to those it gets from administrative agencies. The courts are unlikely to destroy product liability with one sweeping blow, but may be willing to tinker at such things as punitive damages, joint and several liability, and the extent to which liability can be based on technology that didn't exist at the time the product was manufactured. Tinkering, in fact, is all that even the most wildly optimistic business lobbyists have hoped to achieve in the product liability reform bills that have been introduced in Congress.

Reforming product liability law, then, first requires an understanding of the power of courts and an understanding of how the courts themselves can be used to achieve major product liability reform. To put the cart before the horse for a moment, the most intractable problem in product liability law is that it is all local law. Although in the United States manufacturing, employment, markets, and capital flow are national in scope, product liability law is the peculiar creation of each sovereign state. Because there is no national policy on product liability, state courts are usually asked only whether they wish to redistribute some wealth from an out-of-state manufacturer to an injured, in-state plaintiff. The traditional language of the law, speaking as it does about "reasonable risks," "failure to warn," "implied warranties," and "appropriate technology," does a good job obscuring the basic wealth-redistribution question that is asked in state courts. But when product liability cases go to juries, the juries understand the basic question, and usually answer it in a way to please their friends and neighbors. Once the entire product liability issue is stated in terms of interstate wealth transfers, where the decision about transfer is made by the transferees, it is hardly surprising that the law becomes increasingly pro-plaintiff. Judges, of course, are supposed to control the passions of juries, but in product liability the judges often have the same passions as the jurors.

Therefore, if an organized effort to nationalize product liability standards is to have a high likelihood of success, that effort has to be made through the federal courts. The first step in the nationalization process is for business to study both the power of courts and the way business has traditionally responded to that power. Here it is not useful to focus exclusively on the issue of product liability, because product liability is simply one small part of a much larger problem. In fact, as I shall demonstrate in detail later, we can learn much about what the Supreme Court of the United States can do for us in product liability law by studying what the Supreme Court did when it reformed the state criminal law and unified state law on First Amendment, freedom of the press issues in the 1960's; we can learn much more, in fact, than we can learn by studying state or federal product liability cases. The exact same techniques that the federal courts used in criminal and libel law are available for product liability law if the Supreme Court wants to use them. The trick is getting the product liability issue on the Supreme Court's agenda, and to do that business needs a better understanding of what courts can do and how they can do it. Therefore, just for a moment, let's step behind all the obscure legal language and arcane formalities that surround court proceedings and take a look at raw power.

In 1982 the board of education in Logan County, West Virginia, brought an action in the West Virginia Supreme Court of Appeals challenging the way in which a local county assessor levied property taxes. The state constitution provided that property should be assessed "at its true and actual value," but for over a hundred years property had been placed on the tax rolls at about half of its value. In fact, there was a state statute that allowed local assessors to appraise property for tax purposes at 50 percent of market value, and the system had operated in that way for as long as anyone could remember. All the expectations of business concerning the level of property taxes were based on this time-honored custom and usage.

Yet the West Virginia Supreme Court held in favor of the board of education in a 4 to 1 split decision. The effect of this single court ruling was a near doubling of property taxes overnight. The majority of the court were persuaded that the counties desperately needed additional tax revenues to support public education. The constitutional argument about "true and actual value" simply gave the appellate judges an opportunity to strike a blow for higher levels of community services. The legislature immediately called a special session at which they passed a constitutional resolution, later ratified by the voters, that softened the blow by allowing the new taxes to be implemented over a ten-year period, but the net effect was that four members of a five-member state court accomplished in eight weeks something that the West Virginia legislature could not have accomplished in fifty years. In terms of product liability law reform, such stories show that once courts decide to do something, they can usually get it done regardless of the state of existing law, and regardless, too, of the extent to which the existing state of affairs enjoys broad-based political support.

In 1980, Local 1330 of the United Steel Workers of America sued the United States Steel Corporation in federal district court in Ohio to prevent U.S. Steel from closing its steel mill in Youngstown. The union alleged that, over a period of several years, management had made representations to the workers that if the mill could be made profitable, management would not close it down. Relying on the promise, the employees began to work much harder and permitted management to rearrange shifts and combine jobs in order to improve profits. Both the federal court that heard the case and the court of appeals that reviewed it specifically found that "it is beyond argument that the local management of U.S. Steel's Youngstown plants engaged in an all-out effort to make these two plants profitable in order to prevent their being closed. It is equally obvious that the employees responded wholeheartedly." The employees thought that they had performed their part of the contract and that the court should require U.S. Steel to honor its bargain and keep the plants open.

But both the district court and the court of appeals held against the union and in favor of U.S. Steel. The court of appeals concluded that U.S. Steel was not required to keep plants open because of alleged promises unless those promises had been authorized by the corporate board of directors and the agreement had been acknowledged by the executive boards of the employees' unions. Such a contract, the court held, would have had to be for a stated contract period and for a stated mutual consideration.

The federal court decision in the *U.S. Steel* case follows old, established law, but it ignores a lot of new legal principles in the area of contract law that could as well have been chosen to decide the case in favor of the unions. Certainly the employees showed that they had been euchred into making concessions and working abnormally hard thanks to either a deliberate lie or a grossly negligent misrepresentation. The court of appeals decision was quick and dirty; but if the court of appeals had held in favor of the union, the precedent that such a pro-employee ruling would have opened up endless litigation whenever a plant is to be closed. What a case like *U.S. Steel* tells us about product liability law is that plaintiffs do not always win in court no matter how much sympathy they engender. Courts are really concerned about the health of the economy and they are willing, on occasion, to make some very difficult and apparently heartless decisions to keep the economy efficient over the long term.

The West Virginia tax case and the *U.S. Steel* case arose in widely different contexts: one involved a state court's decision under state law about the appropriate level of taxation, and the other involved a federal court's decision about employees' rights to rely on management promises. But both cases have the capacity to affect business in general to a greater extent than anything either Congress or a state legislature is likely to do. For land-intensive businesses like apartment houses, chemical plants, or timber farms, a doubling of state property taxes in a depressed economy can be the last blow before bankruptcy court. For companies like U.S. Steel— besieged by foreign competition and under pressure from new domestic products and technologies—a court would create a nightmare for employers by holding that legitimate efforts to turn money-losing plants around can create vested contract rights to particular jobs.

In the *U.S. Steel* case, an adverse holding could eviscerate good-faith efforts at management / labor cooperation because anything management said or did might then create an enforceable contract; this, in turn, would severely chill informal communication and reduce the extent to which good-faith but legally unenforceable bargains could be made. In the final analysis, the holding in *U.S. Steel* simply stands for the commonsense, pro-business proposition that there are more good than bad deals based on unenforceable hidden handshakes, so the law must be careful about forcing every deal into the mold of a rigid, legal contract. The *U.S. Steel* decision was a matter of immense *political* importance, but it was argued largely in terms of traditional contract law. Somehow I have the feeling that the lawyers who won the case thought that they had achieved a legal rather than a political victory. Nothing, however, could be farther from the truth.

Both corporate counsel and the businessmen they represent seem to understand that a significant number of their political problems emerge from court decisions rather than from the actions of legislatures, executives, or administrative agencies. Yet, while business often challenges the actions of legislators, executives, or administrative agencies, it accepts the actions of courts with the same equanimity with which it accepts violent acts of nature or precipitous declines in the value of the American dollar. About the only serious efforts that business makes to influence the courts in a political fashion are attempts to get pro-business judges either appointed or elected to the federal and state benches.

Indeed, the pro-business Reagan administration appointed about 250 federal district judges and 75 federal appeals judges by 1988, but those judges simply offset 206 federal district judges and 56 federal appeals judges appointed by the Carter administration. Although business wants as many pro-business judges as possible on the bench, playing the appointment game alone will never carry the day. Business is only one of numerous powerful political constituencies attempting to get their friends on the bench. Business will be no more successful in dominating state and federal courts through favorably disposed personnel than it is in dominating legislatures or administrative agencies through the same means.

Courts are political institutions and—like other political institutions—they can be lobbied and persuaded by factual arguments and good reasoning. The major difference between courts and other political institutions, however, is that it is not usually smart to try to bribe appointed judges. In the other branches of government, however, campaign contributions, speaking honoraria, jobs for wives and relatives, and lavish entertainment are the order of the lobbying day. But courts are watched too closely and are too circumscribed by elaborate canons of ethics to make any traditional lobbying techniques useful. That doesn't mean, however, that there aren't other, legitimate ways of influencing court decisions, and that is what this book is about.

As will become obvious a little later, some of the problems business has in court are directly related to the philosophical biases of the judges. Other business problems are related to the way lawyers practice law and to the incentives we have built into the system to encourage litigation. Still other problems emerge from the way the judiciary is organized and from the incentives different organizational patterns create for rendering anti-business decisions. Therefore, before business can alter the outcome of court decisions, it must first isolate the court-related problem or problems that caused the decision that it wants to alter.

It is unlikely, for example, that a local Ohio state court would have given the same answer in the *U.S. Steel* case that the federal court gave, because local Ohio trial court judges are elected and U.S. Steel doesn't have any votes. This, in fact, is one part of the basic problem we have in product liability: the plaintiffs in product liability cases usually are local individuals, and the defendants are usually out-of-state corporations. Consequently, because product liability cases are tried in local courts, the definition of the "community" that the judicial system is designed to protect is very narrowly drawn. This not only affects the "home cooking" aspects of the trial of individual cases, it also affects the formal legal rules governing liability, evidence, procedure, and damages. The law of product liability would probably be altered significantly, however, if the community that the court envisages itself as serving were expanded to include as constituents the defendant's employees, retired pensioners, suppliers, distributors, and even shareholders.

Ironically, it is only in the judiciary that business hopes for politically favorable results by getting favorably disposed individuals appointed or elected. Business, when it deals with legislators or executives, concentrates on co-opting officeholders *after* they have gotten their jobs. Once, I was running in a primary election for the state legislature, and I asked the management of the local Westinghouse plant if I could go through their plant and shake the workers' hands as they left the building. I received a cold, bureaucratic reply full of information concerning Westinghouse's *policy* that forbade active political campaigning by outsiders on plant property, etc., etc.

Nonetheless, I won the election handily, and no sooner did I arrive at the State Capitol than I was deluged with lobbying requests from Westinghouse. Westinghouse management were pleased to take me to dinner, sit for hours laughing at my jokes, or devote time to telling me that I was the smartest human ever to serve in the legislature. Certainly at that point I could have exacted a promise from them that I could tour their plant in the next election: with regard to their "standard policy" they were a bunch of lying hypocrites! Like most professional politicians, however, I never dwelled on who was against me in the *last* election: I was interested only in who was going to be against me in the next one. Westinghouse knew this, and they understood perfectly well that supporting politicians when contests are in doubt is not nearly as efficient as "schmoozing" or "buying" them into cooperation once they are firmly in place.

Of course, for the great majority of politicians who are more or less honest, what the schmoozing and buying actually purchase is access rather than a solid vote. After all, years of PAC contributions, entertainment, speaking honoraria, and schmoozing didn't save business from the ravages of the 1986 tax reform act. In the legislative process the thing that business usually wants is for nothing to happen, and since nothing is what most legislatures are set up to do anyway, it often looks like business has more influence than it actually has.

In February 1987 Senate majority leader Robert C. Byrd was in the eye of a small public relations storm because he offered lobbyists the privilege of having breakfast with him for $10,000 apiece. Robert Byrd will be targeted in 1988 when he runs for reelection to the U.S. Senate *because* he is Senate majority leader. Such targeting means that Robert Byrd will need some money. Those of us who put up with elections all the time find a certain charm in Senator Byrd's having set up a kiosk to sell breakfast tickets at a fixed, up-front price. That way everyone knows exactly where he stands. In fact, I envy Robert Byrd, because no one ever wants to have breakfast with me, even without buying a ticket! Yet the five-member court on which I sit makes more business policy per person than the members of the West Virginia State Senate who get schmoozed from morning till night. I get invitations to big meetings and terrible public dinners, but I would rather stay home teaching my son the hortatory subjunctive of irregular Latin verbs than I would listening to an evening of bad jokes and inarticulate altar calls. Nonetheless, if business executives, NOW officers, or AFL-CIO leaders are not lobbying me about a *specific* case in our court, I'm happy to have breakfast with them and listen to their problems exactly as I did when a member of the legislature.

Like most judges in my position, I want and need information— and that information is of a type that can't be presented in the context of individual cases because it is background information about how the world operates. What, for example, does a steel mill really look like? How do workers on the shop floor respond to management promises? What will companies like U.S. Steel do when they become USX, and how will the "X" factor affect American employment? What do rural public schools look like? What is the correlation between money and quality education? Are we better off giving more money evenhandedly to all schools, or should we build a limited number of lighthouse schools? Former politicians who have been issued black robes and Latin dictionaries should be just as interested in "political" matters *after* they become judges as they were when they held other offices. As both the tax assessment case and the *U.S. Steel* case demonstrate, judges make political decisions—whether we like it or not—and as long as they undertake to perform that function they should do it well rather than badly. Doing it well, in turn, requires lots of information, and good staff work, from people who elsewhere would be called "lobbyists."

The lawmaking power of courts comes from three sources: (1) their power to interpret federal and state constitutions and federal and state statutes; (2) their power to alter the age-old body of uncodified, decisional law (often called the "common law") that governs such business-related matters as contracts and torts; and (3) their power to review administrative agency decisions and substitute their judgment for that of administrators. Put all of those powers together and you have the tail of the courts wagging the dog of legislatures, executives, and administrative agencies. Business, however, currently spends roughly 90 percent of its political resources on 50 percent of its political problems. The other 50 percent of its political problems emerge from the courts, and if business knew a little more about how they operate, it would probably reallocate its political resources. In fact, the liberal constituencies currently devote a high percentage of their political resources to court, possibly because they have little hope of being successful in legislatures.

Ironically, although business spends much time lobbying legislators and executives, legislators and executives aid and abet the gradual accretion of power to the courts, because when courts take over any issue—raising taxes, for example—the court decision takes the political monkey off the backs of elected officeholders. (This, by the way, is what happened when the New Jersey supreme court ordered the legislature to pass an income tax to support the public schools.) Politicians figure that the courts can take the heat for unpopular decisions because all federal judges and many state judges don't need to run for office. What elected politician in his or her right mind wants responsibility for controversial issues like raising taxes, integrating schools, or banning God from public life? "Courts, be our guests," they say, "but, by the way, we all reserve the right to call you dirty sons of bitches all the time, to add credibility to our disclaimer of responsibility for your actions!"

If elected politicians shed only crocodile tears over the increasing power of courts, the average voter is even less concerned. The nonchalance proceeds directly from the love / hate relationship that Americans have always had with democracy. Americans love democracy but hate the politicians who make democracy work. George Washington's warnings about the dangers of political parties, our extensive job-tenured civil service system, the populist devices of referendum and initiative, and the recently enacted limits on campaign spending are examples of our attempts to reduce the extent to which politicians and political coalitions influence political decisions. Judges have had an easy time becoming our supreme political actors because, in an atmosphere in which politicians are severely distrusted and disliked, the politicians who have the most power are the ones who best disguise the fact that they are politicians at all. Judges appear to be honest, objective, nonpartisan, disinterested policymakers: their broadly based political support arises from their apparent separation from influence by well-financed special interests.

Yet the decisions that courts make are just as political as those made elsewhere in government, and require the same type of information about costs and benefits that would instruct the understanding of either legislators or executives. In fact, product liability law is a good example of a major political undertaking that has been engineered with only limited information-gathering on a systematic basis. Business has directed most of its informational resources in its battles over product liability to Congress and the state legislatures. For some reason that I cannot fathom, business has writen off the courts as potential instruments for product liability reform. Yet the fact that the courts produced product liability law out of whole cloth in the first place does not mean that the courts would not like to refine the system to make it better.

Judges are no more eager to bungle an undertaking than other politicians, and if something is broken, they are usually willing to try to mend it. In fact, we see this tendency in operation today with regard to the criminal law. Many pro-defendant rulings of the U.S. Supreme Court made in the 1970's are now being overturned and criminal law is becoming just one or two notches more conservative. Although I share with business generally a pessimistic view of the likelihood of liability reform emerging from state courts, I think that the federal courts hold out positive possibilities far beyond the wildest dreams of business lobbyists in Congress. The courts have been overlooked as agents of tort reform, however, for the simple reason that courts are largely a mystery to the average businessman and his public affairs staff.

Court rulings are reported by the media in the same dispassionate tones that they report professional sports or palace coups in distant lands, but there is little attention to the why or how of court decisions. The big-time media are primarily in the entertainment business; court proceedings are so excruciatingly boring that they have no entertainment value whatsoever. Daily papers and TV networks, then, cannot devote valuable space or time to courts—a subject that evokes only yawns from most readers or viewers. In fact, Jesse Jackson's hopeless bid for the presidency in 1984 received incalculably more media attention than the combined courts of the United States had received in the preceding four years. Jesse Jackson is interesting but not powerful; courts are powerful but not interesting.

Furthermore, judges and lawyers understand that the way to avoid the eagle eye of the press is to keep everything in court so bland and technical that it is totally devoid of any human interest potential. The worst thing that can happen to any court is for the judge to become a media hotdog. When I was thirty-five years old, and had been a judge for four years, I was invited to attend a small conference at the Aspen Institute. The conference was funded by the Ford Foundation, and one of the participants was then Chief Justice Warren Burger. Justice Burger reiterated time and time again that judges should never talk to the press or issue public statements. I still remember every word as he pointed out that the press can only do a judge harm by twisting his words or ridiculing his off-the-cuff remarks. It is enough, he said, for a court to speak through its orders and published opinions. It took me another ten years fully to appreciate the sagacity of that advice, but among high-level judges the chief justice's approach is the "school solution."

Powerful judges are so obscure that few lawyers of my acquaintance can name all the supreme court justices with ease. It is a rare business executive who is able to name more than two members of his local federal court of appeals or his state's highest court. Yet the courts are the most significant political hazard for many enterprises, both large and small. Court modifications of traditional landlord and tenant law can raise the cost of operating an apartment building by as much as 15 percent, and court decisions in the emerging law of "unlawful discharge" can completely rearrange a firm's relationships with its nonunion employees. In short, the power of courts is awesome, but the internal workings of courts are a complete mystery to all except the small number of lawyers who go to court on a regular basis.

The primary reason why courts have been successful in keeping themselves obscure while constantly increasing their political power is that most of what courts do really *is* technical. Although the greatest problems businesses face in court are political and not legal, that is not to say that there are no such things as legal problems. Indeed, there are real legal problems: among them are the formalities necessary for a valid will; the proper clauses to insert into a long-term lease; and the effect of unforeseeable events like a foreign war, or a trade embargo, on a supplier's obligation under a long-term contract. But product liability cases, plant shutdown cases, and tax assessment cases like the one in West Virginia present political problems and not narrow, technical, legal problems.

When we talk about the law of wills, leases, or long-term contracts, everyone agrees on what the law is. Craftsmanship in drafting legal documents involves making the clauses conform to existing legal rules; craftsmanship in litigating routine legal matters involves showing how the facts of a client's case fit existing law. But in product liability cases, plant shutdown cases, and state tax assessment cases, the law is as fluid as Lake Michigan. The basic question in those cases is not how to conform one's actions out-of-court, or produce evidence in-court to meet the requirements of the law, but rather what the law ought to be. When the courts are making new law of general application, the issues that they are considering are "political" issues in the broadest sense of the word.

The number of cases that American courts hear each year is increasing all the time. This expansion in court matters is far in excess of any increase in population: it bespeaks not only more complicated relationships that invite litigation, but also the shift in the center of political power in the direction of the courts.

Americans have gotten used to courts' deciding hot controversies that other branches of government are reluctant to decide, and the more we get used to courts exercising political power, the more they are invited to do so. In response to the increase in case filings, we have not only increased the number of judges, but we have also reorganized the courts to make them more efficient. Among other things, we have given judges several law clerks apiece, reduced from twelve to six the number of persons required for a civil jury, and increased the number of special masters, court commissioners, and bankruptcy judges who stand in for general jurisdiction judges in certain types of proceedings.

The expansion of court capacity has, in turn, significantly increased the overall hazard to which business is exposed in the courts. Yet the strength of the courts, politically, is directly related to the ironic phenomenon that the people who most consistently vilify the courts are also the first to use them for political purposes. Business, for example, goes to court at the first sign of an adverse decision by an administrative agency. But the adversaries of business—environmentalists, for instance—use the courts to twist business into knots whenever business wants a new coal mine, downtown development, or factory. Strident complaints by business about the judicial jeopardy to which it is exposed often obscure the fact that business is more often the aggressor than the victim in the court process that controls administrative agencies. The bottom line, therefore, is that although business has well-justified complaints about some of the decisions that courts make, business needs the courts as much as do the minorities, accident victims, and environmentalists whom we usually think of as being the primary beneficiaries of the courts' largesse.

In fact, much of the success of American business is directly related to the power and independence of American courts. Throughout our history it has been the courts that have protected business from government. All during the nineteenth century the federal courts worked diligently to establish an internal free trade zone among the American states by striking down local legislation that discriminated against interstate commerce. At the same time, the courts created an elaborate commercial law to facilitate trade among strangers in distant cities. This, perhaps, was the first exercise in judicial activism by American courts, and it was loudly applauded by business. Today it is the courts that guarantee that private property will not be taken for public use without just compensation, and it is the courts that shield business from over-zealous regulators. One reason that America is able to borrow so much money from abroad with only modest interest rate differentials is that we have become the world's safe-deposit box. Foreigners have faith that American courts will protect their investments in the United States, which makes America the resting place of choice for hot money acquired by hook or by crook in the rest of the world.

The least sophisticated approach, then, that business can take to its court-related problems is simply to complain loudly that "the courts are doing too much." This may be psychologically satisfying, but it can't possibly translate into any serious political program. At the simplest level, the same businessman who complains that courts are doing too much is probably in favor of doubling the number of bankruptcy judges, because all business matters touching an insolvent debtor's estate quickly grind to a screeching halt owing to the current congestion in bankruptcy courts. Yet today's bankruptcy judges have powers over debtors' estates that would have been considered absolutely astonishing as recently as twenty years ago.

The truth of the matter is that business has a variety of different types of problems in court, each of which requires a custom-crafted solution. From its point of view, in some instances—such as the power to create new product liability law—the courts are too powerful. But in other instances, such as bankruptcy proceedings, the courts are not powerful enough, because they are crippled by lack of manpower and by overly complicated procedures. Furthermore, many of business's problems in the courts have little or nothing to do with the courts themselves. For example, each year American law schools turn out roughly 35,000 new graduates, most of whom will eventually be licensed to practice law. This number, however, far exceeds either replacement requirements for lawyers who retire or the natural expansion of legal business.

Lawyers, unfortunately, are not a passive commodity like surplus corn or cheese; they vindicate Say's law that supply will create its own demand. As thousands of lawyers are released on American society with bleak prospects for steady employment, it is inevitable that clients with weaker and weaker cases will be able to find lawyers willing to represent them for contingent fees. And as we get farther and farther away from the golden era for lawyers that spanned the decade from 1967 to 1977, when the proliferation of federal and state regulations opened up hundreds of thousands of new lawyer jobs, fewer and fewer brilliant undergraduates will choose law school over competing graduate programs.

About 30 percent of American law schools are now back to an "open admissions" policy, which simply means that any college graduate who can pay the tuition will be accepted. Gone are the days when every law school had three qualified applicants for every place and admission requirements were rigorous. In 1986, West Virginia University's College of Law reduced its class size by 40 percent to sustain the quality of its graduates. Most schools, however, are not allowed that luxury; they have tenured faculty to employ, debts to repay, and community expectations to meet. The increasing surplus of poorly qualified law school graduates bodes ill for business because the number of frivolous lawsuits is destined to rise. A bunch of dumb lawyers are more likely to be ambulance chasers than they are to crowd the more intellectually demanding fields of taxation, administrative law, or corporate takeovers.

It should be obvious that simply reducing the power of courts (the least sophisticated approach), or getting pro-business judges appointed or elected (the next sophisticated approach), will not necessarily take care of an increasing volume of frivolous lawsuits. The current system encourages lawsuits because there are no penalties for filing weak claims. In a system where each side pays its own lawyers' fees, plaintiffs are not discouraged from placing their grievances in the hands of lawyers working for contingent fees, and, if lawyers are not busy, they have no disincentive to filing suits that might elicit modest settlement offers simply because of their nuisance value. Even a blind hog gets an acorn occasionally, and it's possible to operate a low-key, low overhead plaintiffs' practice on that basic principle.[1]

It is even possible to make a case that some of the court-related problems experienced by business are directly related to the way business's own law firms are set up. Lawyers are in the litigation business and not in the quick, cheap settlement business: for busi-

---

1. Yet tinkering at the current system where everyone pays his own lawyer may do business more harm than good. Currently many legitimate but small claims against business simply get written off by plaintiffs because it costs too much to go to court. Consequently, there has never been a concerted effort on the part of business lawyers to change the system. Business does not want to be stuck both with judgments *and* the other side's lawyers' fees.

ness lawyers to make money there must be a lot of billable hours devoted to lawyers' dancing around before a final settlement is struck. Senior partners in large firms make money buying young lawyers at wholesale and selling them at retail. In the large defense firms young lawyers earn over $50,000 a year, but they are expected to bill at least 2,000 hours of work to clients every year. Forty hours of *billable* time a week in a fifty-week work year translates into about sixty-two hours a week in the office. My own former clerks who have gone to big firms are utterly amazed by the lack of supervision they receive on projects that involve scores of millions of dollars. Big firms just release expensive young lawyers to process paper—like blizzards of pretrial motions and discovery requests—and let their meters click along accordingly.

After years of working with young lawyers I suspect that about 40 percent of the billable hours of young associates are devoted to the legal equivalent of reinventing the wheel. For big business, even outrageous legal fees are an insignificant component of total costs, but for small business simply defending lawsuits in today's big-firm system may be a financial nightmare. None of this, however, relates directly to the courts. These business law-firm dynamics would prevail regardless of whether the courts had less political power, and regardless of whether a host of pro-business judges ascended the bench.

There are also court-related problems that proceed directly from ribald, freewheeling politics rather than from the organization of the courts or specific rules of law. In twenty-two states all of the judges are elected, and in about half of the other states judges must face some type of retention election even if they are appointed initially. Obviously, in any elected system there is a strong temptation to decide cases in favor of the local folks who vote, rather than in favor of the out-of-state folks who do not. State judicial races (particularly at the appellate level where elections are statewide) are increasingly becoming high-profile, high-cost, media events. When this occurs, judges must raise money from somebody. Unfortunately, it is a rare judge who is so well loved that he can raise money from everyone in an evenhanded way. In fact, well-loved judges can't raise money from anyone at all. Litigants don't want judges who will be intelligent and fair; litigants want judges who will decide cases their way.

In 1984 I ran for reelection to the state supreme court in a four-man Democrat primary. There was no Republican opposition in the general election. The ballot allowed the voter to vote for two candidates out of an undifferentiated field of four, which meant that the two highest vote-getters won. One of my opponents, a colleague on our court, had a strong "liberal" record. For the preceding eight years the court had been activist in a "liberal" direction, and had come under heavy criticism from middle-of-the-road Democrat politicians, the business community, and conservatives. The second of my opponents was a former state senate president who was supported by business and the conservatives. He ran as a judicial traditionalist, and in spite of the fact that he had been a "liberal" state legislator, he was the "conservative" candidate in the 1984 judicial race because he appeared to be an electable alternative to a group of radicals. My third opponent was a volunteer with no organized support. He ran fourth and carried only a few counties close to his home.

The irony of my own situation was that *both* the liberal candidate and the conservative candidate raised significantly more money than I did! The liberals found me acceptable, but did not look on me as their die-hard advocate, and the conservatives felt exactly the same way. I had dissented from a number of the court's important activist decisions (like the tax assessment case I described earlier), so that by 1984 I was thought of as the most conservative member of the court. Ironically, this contrasted sharply with my reputation during my first four years on the court, when I was generally regarded as its most liberal member. I had not changed, but the court had. My financial statement conclusively showed that no one liked me very much. Apparently I had not done anything for anybody *lately*.

As it turned out, I led the ticket, but only because I was everyone's *second* choice. My inherited name recognition and years of spadework speaking at civic functions and ushering school tours through the state supreme court probably saved me, but I would not want to run in such an election again. Where judges are elected and a court has high visibility, the judge who courts no special interest and assumes no ideological posture is at a severe disadvantage. Well-regarded, "fair" judges make no friends at all among well-financed vested interests, which means that they'll come up short in the fund-raising business. In the final analysis, it is the media blitz, and not one's reputation among lawyers and knowledgeable laymen, that wins judicial elections these days.

Because most of the routine litigation concerning business takes place in state rather than federal courts, the way in which state judges get their jobs has a major impact on the outcome of lawsuits. I have known many judges of both left- and right-wing political persuasions who decide cases on the captions. Among left-wing judges, if the case's caption reads *Individual v. Insurance Company,* the Individual wins for no better reason than that he is the little guy taking on a big corporation. If the case is captioned *Employee v. Employer,* and the question is race or sex discrimination, the Employee wins regardless of how fair and nondiscriminatory the employer has been, just because such a holding is politically fashionable. The right-wing judges, of course, are a businessman's dream: they also decide cases on the captions, but the winners and losers are reversed. Furthermore, although elected courts are the ones that lend themselves most easily to a political rather than a judicial mentality, the tendency to decide cases on the captions can also be found in the federal courts and in the appointed state courts. Both presidents and governors go out looking for judicial candidates to appoint who have track records of being on their political side. Ronald Reagan has deliberately sought out militantly conservative judicial nominees, just as Jimmy Carter sought out militantly liberal nominees. These leopards seldom change their spots once elevated to the bench.

In the elected systems, judges are likely to brag publicly that they are "the people's judge" or "the AFL-CIO judge," because they must generate militant election-day support. In the appointed systems—both federal and state—the political judges can afford to be quieter about their biases, but biases still exist from a lifetime's worth of political partisanship. When, therefore, business gets into the hands of a radically anti-business trial court judge, it is in serious trouble unless it can find a sympathetic appeals panel to which it can go at an early stage of the proceedings. This is particularly the case in mass tort litigation, where hundreds or even thousands of suits against several defendants are consolidated before one trial court judge.

The purpose of this horseback ride through some of the salient features of courts is to point out that the problems that businesses encounter in courts are not the result of one simple structural imperfection. Part of those problems relate directly to a wholesale shift in the center of political power in the direction of the courts. Another part comes from the sheer number of lawyers that are graduated every year from mediocre law schools, and even from the way business manages its own law firms. Finally, business has political problems that center in the way judges are elected or appointed.

In product liability law the entire field is dominated by court decisions. These decisions, in turn, emerge from a judicial system in which injured local plaintiffs sue large, out-of-state corporations before local juries, in local courts, under the direction of local trial and appellate judges. Unlike environmental matters, where a court must evaluate the proper balance between employment and a clean environment for the *same constituency,* in product liability cases a judgment for the plaintiff helps the home team while the adverse effects of that judgment are felt entirely by the visiting team. In environmental matters a court is as likely to help business as it is to hinder business: in product liability, however, the insular nature of the decision-making structure always ensures that business will come off as the villain when the jury returns from its deliberations.

Therefore, when we are talking about improving the performance of business in court, there is no such thing as a general, broad-based approach. Court-related problems in America's business affairs are like disease in the human body: there is not just one potential disease, but rather a host of potential diseases. Each disease, in turn, requires a specific cure. And, to carry the analogy one step farther, the cure for one disease may itself either cause or aggravate another disease. Chemotherapy may cure cancer, but it makes your hair fall out and causes unrelenting nausea for several days after treatment. Marijuana may make you listless and blow your mind as a teenager, but it works wonders overcoming the nausea caused by chemotherapy. In medicine, diseases and their cures are very specific, and for a medical treatise to be useful it must be narrowly focused. I have concluded that the same applies to business and its relationship to the courts.

Mine is a book primarily about reducing the hazards faced by business in the area of product liability. However, it is not a book about what the rules governing product liability law ought to be, nor is it a diatribe about the inequities that product liability law has caused. Rather, it is a book about how the uncoordinated American federal structure, with its fifty-three separate systems of courts, inevitably leads to results unnecessarily adverse to business interests in product liability cases. It is also about how business can change the court structure that often renders such perverse results in these cases, and how by changing that structure the over-all in-court and out-of-court results will inevitably change. From the most practical point of view possible, the best thing that business can do to improve its posture in the product liability area is to work to change the structure of the *system* from which product liability law emerges. As I shall demonstrate at length in the last chapter, it is a waste of time to try to get specific changes in existing law out of the same old moth-eaten system.

Fortunately, the issue of product liability law is a special case within a larger, general case. The general case relates to the whole problem of legal chaos produced by a federal system where we have numerous, uncoordinated, separate state court systems competing among themselves for power over the same subject matter. The larger general case bodes well for business, because it means that there are some powerful allies who can be enlisted in an over-all program of reform. In fact, the most widespread and egregious examples of the general case occur in the law of domestic relations, which means that potentially the entire feminist lobby can be enlisted to support any efforts that business initiates to unify or generally tighten up the current sprawling mass of chaotic state law.

Although the central focus of my concern is the product liability law that affects business, I have decided to present most of the rest of this book in terms of the general case, rather than just in terms of the special case of product liability law. By dealing with the general case it is possible to broaden the base of support for law unification. Suggesting greater law uniformity under the direction of the federal courts takes the proponent into political "Indian country," a problem that will be discussed at length in Chapter 5. Business, therefore, will need as many allies as possible if it is to make a successful—if very limited—challenge to the current, decentralized federal system. It is my hope that explaining the details of the general case will help business become better equipped to enlist those allies.

What follows, then, is an analysis in the broadest possible context of the system that has produced product liability law. All efforts up to this point to tinker at local product liability law through national legislation have been dismal failures. Furthermore, with the reduction in conservative momentum in the wake of Ronald Reagan's imminent departure from office, it is unlikely that the Congress will be more favorable to product liability legislation in the future than it has been in the past. No matter: I want to demonstrate that congressional action is neither necessary nor desirable as the best way to solve the product liability problem.

Simply by consigning to federal courts supervision the broad outline of product liability law, we can dramatically change the nature of the "community" that is going to make product liability decisions. And once the Supreme Court of the United States, and the lower federal courts, put liability law on their agenda, there is a significant likelihood that the federal courts will achieve at one stroke what business has been vainly trying to do in Congress for the last decade. To do that successfully, however, business must understand the entire general case of legal chaos, and so it is to an exploration of that general case that we now turn.

Chapter 2

The Uncommon Law

American lawyers are fond of pointing out that the United States is a "common-law" country. By that they usually mean that American law, like early English law, relies more on judge-made rules than it does on legislative codes. But to use the term "common law" simply to refer to a malleable, court-dominated legal system misses what was perhaps the most important feature of the original common law—namely, its uniformity.

When William the Conqueror landed in England he found a country that was governed by a great variety of local customs. Over the next three hundred years the Norman kings succeeded in establishing one uniform system of laws through the use of itinerant royal judges who were professional administrators of the law, all trained in one school. In the context of English law, use of the word "common," then, does not mean "ordinary" or "vulgar," but rather "uniform."

America, however, has turned the common law on its head. When we refer to ourselves as a "common-law" country we have slipped behind the looking glass, because the United States has very little uniform, national law. Unlike England, with its centralized court system staffed by a cadre of similarly trained judges, the United States today has fifty-three separate court systems. First, there is the nationwide system of federal courts, which is divided into thirteen separate circuits that are loosely held together by the Supreme Court of the United States. In addition to the federal system, however, there are freestanding court systems in the fifty states, the District of Columbia, and Puerto Rico. The U.S. Supreme Court hears appeals from state courts,[1] but it does so only in cases involving an issue of federal law. Most state court cases present no federal law issues. In over fifteen years on West Virginia's highest court, I can remember only three of our cases being accepted for review by the U.S. Supreme Court.

America's diversity of *court systems* leads to a diversity of *law systems* because American judges, like their English predecessors, have extensive lawmaking powers. And because each separate court system is administratively independent, each can generate eccentric judge-made law at odds with the statutory and judge-made law of other jurisdictions. Whole fields of American law, such as contracts and torts, are creatures of court decisions rather than legislative enactments. (In some states, like Pennsylvania, even the crime of murder is not defined by statute, because the definition of murder is so well settled by court decisions that a code definition is unnecessary.) Ironically, then, although business is increasingly national in nature, most of the law that governs business is parochial state tort, contract, or property law that not only guides decisions in local state courts, but also binds local federal judges when they are called upon to decide lawsuits based on state law between citizens of different states.[2]

Today's separate court systems are simply the product of history: the United States began as a union of *sovereign* states. Our politicians are still fond of calling us "*these* United States," instead of "*The* United States," but few people today feel a stronger allegiance to a state than they feel to the country as a whole. This was not always the case: when I was a child many southerners still thought of themselves as citizens of a conquered nation. (My own grandfather was expelled from the West Virginia University College of Law for whistling "Dixie" on campus.) Certainly at the time of our constitutional convention in 1787 the states were jealous of their sovereignty.

Because the original thirteen American states were originally

1. Hereafter I shall lump the state-like courts of the District of Columbia and Puerto Rico with the courts of the fifty states because, for the purposes of this book, they present exactly the same structural problems concerning lack of uniformity.

2. These state-based claims—tried in federal court only because of diversity of citizenship—are called "diversity cases."

set up as sovereign nations, each state today has most of the government machinery of a miniature country. In 1789 the national government probably couldn't have run the country even if the *Constitution* had empowered it to do so. If, for example, John Adams had wanted to visit a friend in South Carolina, he would have had to go by ship; it would have taken at least ten days in good weather; and the trip would have been more perilous than flying 200,000 miles on today's airlines. In 1789 we really were "*these* United States." Consequently, the courts of each state resemble the entire English court system at the time of the American Revolution, and each state's courts have roughly the same powers that the courts of England had in 1776.

In the *Constitution of the United States* there are but two clauses that attempt to tie America's courts together. The first provides that the laws of the federal government shall be supreme throughout the land and that state courts must enforce federal law. The second provides that the judgments of the courts of any one state shall be given "full faith and credit" in other states. The "supremacy clause" dealing with the superior authority of federal law is reasonably easy to apply and is carefully followed. The full faith and credit clause, however, is like unto a lawyers' full-employment act; it is honored sporadically and capriciously at best.

Try as a divorced father, for example, to use a valid Ohio court custody decree to get your child away from its maternal grandparents in California. California might give you the child because the judge thinks you'll be a good parent, but the Ohio decree is not binding on the California court. When faced with an out-of-state custody decree that affects a resident child, California (or any other state) will apply its own conclusions about what's best for the child, and the out-of-state court be damned. Even enforcing an out-of-state money judgment in a contract case isn't simple, because a state court will allow the defendant to challenge the jurisdiction of the other state's court. Although a successful action may eventually be brought on an out-of-state judgment, it can be a long and needlessly expensive process.

America's competitors are not confronted by inconsistent, uncoordinated courts within their own countries. The Japanese, for example, conceive of themselves as a nation in which individuals must submerge their own interests to further community harmony. Japan has fewer than six thousand lawyers to serve a population greater than half our own, and litigation of any type is rare.

But the law that governs Japan is a tightly knit body of formal and informal national rules that are easily understood (at least by the Japanese), and consistently administered. England and France have extensive litigation, but all litigation in those countries is conducted in one national court system in which consistent rules are applied by centralized courts of appeals. In the United States, however, a person can be in court for years without getting conclusive results, merely because one state court system refuses to recognize decisions from another state court system.

For example, in 1982 both Texas and California levied inheritance taxes on Howard Hughes' billion-dollar-plus estate, claiming that at the time of his death Mr. Hughes was a resident of their respective states. Obviously, an estate the size of Howard Hughes' presented more than just personal problems for heirs; the Hughes estate presented significant business problems for numerous corporations. Management in Hughes-controlled companies knew neither who would end up owning what, nor the management philosophy of the new owners. Until the taxes were determined, no one knew what would need to be sold, or under what terms. The administrator of the Hughes estate was willing to concede that Mr. Hughes was a resident of either Texas or California, but he did not intend to stand still while both states decided that Mr. Hughes and his money belonged to them!

Under universally accepted American law, a person can be a resident of only one state. Yet, in our chaotic system, it could easily be determined by the Texas courts that Howard Hughes was a resident of Texas, and by the California courts that he was a resident of California. In other words, each state could conclude independently, in its own court system, that Mr. Hughes had met its residency requirements. The administrator of the Hughes estate decided that, because the United States is, after all, one country, he would ask the federal courts to sort out his problem and tell everyone in which state Howard Hughes lived. One would expect the *Constitution of the United States* to somehow provide a plan for relief in situations like this, but neither the "supremacy clause" nor the "full faith and credit clause" was of any avail.

When the Hughes case went to the Supreme Court of the United States, the Court held that there was no federal jurisdiction to decide the matter—which was tantamount to giving either Texas or California a license to loot the Hughes estate. Yet it is easy to understand why the U.S. Supreme Court decided not to expand federal jurisdiction to encompass this type of case. Although Howard Hughes' estate is a unique matter in terms of both the decedent's money and notorious eccentricities, the jurisdictional problem is typical of thousands of cases involving competing state claims that arise every year. Welcoming the Hughes estate problem into federal court, and crafting a new legal theory on which relief could be given, would have invited a *tsunami* of similar cases involving less interesting people and much less money.

The case that best illustrates helter-skelter, uncoordinated law in the United States, however, is the fiasco involving Texaco and Pennzoil. As of the fall of 1987 the Texaco case had been in a Texas state trial court, a Texas intermediate court of appeals, the Texas supreme court, a federal district court in New York, the Federal Court of Appeals for the Second Circuit, the Supreme Court of the United States, and a federal bankruptcy court in New York. Pennzoil recovered a Texas state court judgment against Texaco for $10.53 billion plus prejudgment interest, of which $3 billion were punitive damages.

Texaco is America's third largest oil company and its eighth largest corporation: it has assets of $34 billion, liabilities of $20 billion, operations in 150 separate nations, and annual revenues in excess of $32.6 billion. Given that Texaco's yearly revenues exceed the gross national product of 25 percent of the world's independent nation-states, how its problems are treated in the courts of the United States is a matter of no small consequence to a lot of people besides Texaco's directors and its shareholders.

Texaco's joyride through the fun house of American law began in 1984 when it successfully outbid Pennzoil for the assets of Getty Oil. Originally, Getty's management and one stockholder, Gordon Getty, who controlled 40 percent of Getty stock through a family trust, agreed with Pennzoil to a complicated deal by which Getty Oil would be taken private. Pennzoil would buy half the shares that Gordon Getty did not control, and Getty Oil itself would buy back the rest. Pennzoil would then own three-sevenths of the reconstituted company (an interest equivalent to a billion barrels of oil), and the trust that Gordon Getty controlled would then own four-sevenths.

Texaco, however, looked with lust on Getty's rich oil reserves, so, before the deal with Pennzoil was completed, Texaco offered $125 per share for all the Getty stock. Gordon Getty's trust (owning 40 percent of the stock) jumped at the deal, and so Texaco bought Getty right out from under Pennzoil. Mr. J. Hugh Liedtke, CEO of Pennzoil, then said: "We're going to sue everybody in sight"—and that's exactly what happened.

Owing to the peculiarities of state corporation law, both Texaco and Pennzoil are nominally Delaware corporations. Although its principal place of business was originally in Texas, Texaco long ago stopped wearing cowboy boots and ten-gallon hats, moved its corporate headquarters to the suburbs of New York City, and tried very hard to forget its humble origins in the Texas boondocks. Pennzoil, on the other hand, continues to maintain its corporate headquarters in Houston. And so it came to pass that Pennzoil sued Texaco in a friendly, hometown, Texas state trial court.

The fact that both Texaco and Pennzoil are incorporated in Delaware defeated grounds for diversity jurisdiction in federal court, so it was in Houston, among Pennzoil's friends, at the hands of a local Texas jury, that judgment against Texaco for $10.53 billion was entered in 1985. It seems to me, after fifteen years as a judge, that the measure of damages used by the Texas trial court confounds just about every generally accepted principle of the law of damages in the United States. Of the $10.53 billion, $7.53 billion was awarded on the basis of what it would cost Pennzoil to recover one billion barrels of oil over the next 25 years by drilling for it.

The popular business press has tended to focus on the legal rules governing the award of damages in *Pennzoil v. Texaco*. I, however, would go further. The *Texaco* case was allegedly tried under principles of New York law, and the gravamen of Pennzoil's action against Texaco was tortious interference with an existing contract. The Texas intermediate appellate court wrote an opinion substantially affirming the Texas trial court, yet clearly showing in its own citations that Texaco did nothing wrong: it is very hard for an impartial observer not to conclude that the Texas Court of Appeals decision was not prompted by a surpassing ignorance of the most rudimentary principles of law. Yet, having said this for the record, let us pretend for a moment to take the Texas courts seriously, and follow the case as if it were an exercise in law rather than something else.

Regardless of whether Texaco committed some type of business tort by offering more money to Getty Oil than did Pennzoil, the measure of damages in this case is "utterly outrageous and such that all mankind would exclaim against it at first blush," (one of my favorite common-law standards for whether an appellate court should overturn a jury's award of damages). In fact, it is hard for me to imagine any impartial appellate court that would not feel compelled to reverse the trial court judgment on the issue of damages alone, simply because the jury was not properly instructed on how lost profits were properly to be calculated. Furthermore, the fact that the Supreme Court of Texas refused to review this case leads me to believe that Texas has the most corrupt judicial system in the United States.

For our purposes here, one problem in *Pennzoil v. Texaco* was that Texas has an eccentric local state law that requires a losing defendant to post a bond for the entire amount of a trial court judgment before it can appeal and get a stay preventing its judgment creditor from selling off its assets to satisfy the judgment. In Texaco's case, this meant posting a $13 billion bond, which was impossible for Texaco to do. But if Texaco couldn't post the bond, how was it going to get to the Texas Supreme Court to have the judgment overturned? Under the Texas Constitution's "open courts" clause, the Texas courts could waive the bond requirement, but lawyers for Texaco didn't bother to ask the Texas courts to waive the bond.

The reason that Texaco didn't ask the Texas appellate courts to waive the bond was that Texaco had a little home cooking of its own in mind for Pennzoil. The tasty dish to be served to Pennzoil came out of the oven when Texaco went to a friendly, hometown federal district court in New York where a White Plains federal judge enjoined the Texas courts from enforcing the Texas bond requirement against Texaco, thereby protecting Texaco's assets from an order of execution while Texaco appealed the judgment to the Texas Court of Appeals.[3] Pennzoil, however, appealed this lower federal court decision about the bond to the Federal Court of Appeals for the Second Circuit, which affirmed it, and then to the U.S. Supreme Court where, in March 1987, the Supreme Court reversed the Court of Appeals. The Supreme Court held that there was no federal jurisdiction on the part of the New York federal district court to enjoin the operation of a nondiscriminatory, state court procedural rule in an on-going state court proceedings, at least until it became clear that the state court would violate a clear

---

3. In April 1987 the Texas Intermediate Court of Appeals turned Texaco down, paving the way for Texaco to apply to the Texas Supreme Court. It is this April 1987 opinion that I rank among the worst opinions written in a major case by any state court in this century.

federal right. Because Texaco had not asked the Texas courts to waive the bond requirement, the Supreme Court said that the federal courts must abstain from intervention until Texas acted. At that point an appeal could be taken to the U.S. Supreme Court. Thus, by March 1987 Texaco was back to finding a $13 billion appeal bond, which of course it couldn't do. Texaco offered to settle for $2 billion, but Pennzoil was piggy; serious settlement negotiations then blew up in a deluge of acrimony and abuse, leading Texaco to escalate the battle by seeking refuge in yet another court system.

In April 1987 Texaco, with a net worth of over $13 billion, filed for bankruptcy in federal court, primarily to protect its assets from seizure while prosecuting its appeal to the Texas Supreme Court. Once bankruptcy is declared, a debtor's unsecured creditors cannot levy on the debtor's assets. All creditors are paid according to an orderly plan established by the bankruptcy court. The problem for Texaco, of course, is that it is far easier to get into bankruptcy than it is to get out of it. Among other things, there is the overwhelming physical task of giving individual notice to all of Texaco's creditors. Even with all of Pennzoil's judgment plus accrued interest accepted as valid, Texaco is still solvent, and has net assets in excess of all liabilities.

Despite the fact that so far the *Texaco* case has been in seven different courts, the central issue to be decided is very simple. Texaco was outrageously treated by a local trial court. Now this is a common problem, and it happens everywhere with some regularity, including the high-quality federal courts. That is why we have appellate courts—but the eccentric Texas law on appeal bonds makes it impossible for Texaco to appeal. Thus America's eighth largest corporation, with all that implies in terms of employment, investment, and taxes, is held hostage and completely stymied for three years simply because there is no rational mechanism at the national level to solve a national problem like Texaco's. One jerkwater Texas state trial court (with the obscene concurrence of a Texas court of appeals) has managed to screw up something bigger than many nation-states, and while there is much complaint about the ultimate results, there seems to be no serious questioning of the system that produced such an aberration.

For those unfamiliar with the details of our current system, it probably appears logical that the highest use of federal courts would be to provide uniformity throughout the fifty-two state or state-like court systems, to solve exactly the types of problems that Texaco or the administrator of Howard Hughes' estate has. Certainly, if we wanted to create national law, the obvious vehicle for that purpose would be the federal courts. But the federal courts are not currently used for uniformity purposes. Ironically, most of what federal courts do now is to decide low-level disputes that find their way into federal court either because historically they have been placed there by Congress, or because the quality of federal courts attracts litigants away from other available state court forums. If Texaco had not been unlucky enough to have been a Delaware corporation, it would have been in federal court in the twinkling of an eye when Pennzoil sued, and would probably have been awarded a summary judgment.

All kinds of litigants, both big and small, flock to the federal courts because their professionalism and superior administration appear to produce a better brand of justice. Certainly in federal court Texaco would not have faced unreasonable mechanical obstacles to perfecting an appeal. Yet most of what federal courts currently do could be done in state courts, as the following catalogue of federal court functions will quickly reveal. In fact, if there were proper federal court supervision to reduce the invitations to home cooking, and some national rules about such matters as appeal bonds, even the Texaco case could have been handled properly in state court.

First in the catalogue of federal court functions there are the federal criminal cases, which under the "Speedy Trial Act" take precedence over all federal court civil matters. If a hostile foreign power had deliberately set out to sabotage the American economy by making its court system incompetent, it could not have done a better job than by wasting America's best commercial courts on two-bit criminals. Some prosecutions, of course, are worthy of federal court resources because only the federal courts can establish uniform, nationwide standards on official corruption, antitrust, or financial market fraud. But the vast majority of federal criminals are simply unimaginative, petty villains who could as well be tried by justices of the peace. There is a great difference between prosecutions for official corruption (where federal prosecutors and federal judges are needed because some part of the state machinery— police, prosecutors, or even judges—are in on the take), and prosecutions for armed bank robbery, interstate transport of stolen vehicles, or drug dealing. It should be obvious that a person need not be tried in federal court simply because he broke a federal law. Certainly in the civil law many cases based on federal rights are brought in state court for economy and convenience.

The reason bank robbers, hot-car dealers, and drug pushers get valuable federal court time is that it has always been thought that the federal government has sufficient interest in enforcing its own laws that it should do so in its own courts. But today drug trafficking, bank robbery, and hot cars prominently intrude themselves on to the dockets of America's highest paid, best educated, and most important courts. Furthermore, interest groups that wish to keep the dockets of federal courts clogged (to produce long waiting times that make it easier for defendants to settle lawsuits cheaply) are quite pleased that pedestrian criminal cases take precedence over important civil matters like antitrust cases, class actions, and product liability suits.[4] In fact, in many federal districts, like that for northern West Virginia, the criminal docket is so crowded that there are no judges available at all to provide trials in civil cases.

When the federal courts aren't slogging through trifling criminal trials, they are usually sorting out federal civil rights cases. For anyone raised in the sixties, the term "civil rights case" conjures up images of white knight federal judges protecting the weak and the helpless from the likes of Bull Connor; but today's typical "civil rights case" is nothing but a tort suit against a government-related institution, like a hospital. Historically, the states have enjoyed something called "sovereign immunity," which simply means that they can't be sued under state law for money damages. But after the Civil War, Congress passed a little statute (42 U.S.C. 1983) that prohibited public officials from denying any citizen his civil rights "under color of state law." This statute was passed during reconstruction to protect recently emancipated blacks from being beaten, intimidated, or disfranchised by local white officials; but the statute was little used until the 1960's when it was resurrected by activist federal judges to protect the average citizen from just about every type of outrageous state or local official conduct. Through the fiction of suing a state official rather than the state itself, the restrictions of both the Eleventh Amendment (which

---

4. I have discussed this phenomenon at length in another book. See *Why Courts Don't Work* (New York: McGraw-Hill, 1982).

provides that the *states* shall not be made defendants in federal courts) and of state sovereign immunity are overcome.

Under the Civil Rights Act today, prisoners sue guards for taking away their television sets; doctors sue administrators of state-supported hospitals for revoking hospital privileges; state liquor store employees sue supervisors for firing them; and traffic offenders sue justices of the peace for setting their bonds too high. Civil rights cases have come to play an important (and largely positive) role in our law, but now state judges are as inclined as federal judges to enforce the civil rights law. In fact, civil rights cases are a good example of the type of civil matters that today are voluntarily brought in state courts for convenience and economy. The federal courts, however, are still flooded with these suits.

Finally, the federal courts spend lots of time on ordinary civil lawsuits, like automobile accident and product liability cases, when the parties are citizens of different states. Ostensibly, the reason for giving the federal courts jurisdiction in such cases is to avoid local bias against out-of-state litigants, such as that witnessed in the *Texaco* case. However, the federal courts sitting in diversity cases more often than not apply the state law of the state in which they are sitting, which means that an out-of-state litigant gets no break at all in terms of the law that will be applied to his case. As the next chapter will demonstrate in depth, this is almost always a bigger problem than the type of home cooking, mockery-of-justice problem we find in *Texaco*. Furthermore, federal judges are every bit as local as state judges (although they are not elected, which is often an advantage), and the jury that hears a case in federal court will be drawn entirely from the narrow geographical district in which the federal court sits. This means that federal courts can have almost as great a local bias as any state court, although that bias is significantly diluted at the appellate level.

Despite the possibility of some local bias in federal courts, however, plaintiffs' as well as defendants' lawyers fight tenaciously to keep the federal courts in the diversity business simply because those courts have good judges and are efficiently run. Many state courts, particularly in the big cities, are staffed from top to bottom by political hacks, and attending one of them is like spending a day at the circus. The federal courts, on the other hand, are reasonably well run even in New York and Chicago.

The complaints voiced here about the waste of federal court resources on criminal, civil rights, and diversity cases are hardly new. Federal judges complain all the time about the insignificance of the cases that dominate their dockets, but the public's and the lawyers' response is that federal judges get paid for deciding cases of importance to litigants and not to amuse themselves making grandiose national legal policy. One reason, therefore, that there is no political commitment to rearranging the federal and state courts' jurisdiction is that no one has a clear vision of what federal courts ought to be doing besides deciding criminal, civil rights, and diversity cases.

Howard Hughes' administrator and Texaco's CEO, however, have good ideas about something useful that a federal judge could do for them. Also, an ordinary housewife named Linda Berger could suggest something that a federal judge could do for her that would be more useful than presiding in hot-car cases—namely, he could save her five years of being tossed around like a pin-ball in a bunch of uncoordinated state courts, watching the "No Sale" sign pop up in every court she visited. As Mrs. Berger's case demonstrates, the problems of inconsistent, uncoordinated state courts are not just business problems. Furthermore, they are not limited to instances when a local state court deliberately decides to serve home cooking to an out-of-state defendant, as in *Texaco,* or to instances when inconsistent results are reached over the same matter in different state courts, as in the Hughes estate case. The ordinary citizen, particularly when she is litigating about a domestic problem, is often affected by the sheer structural incom-petence of our uncoordinated system.

Mrs. Berger's case was a routine interstate matter of family law. In 1960 Linda married Martin Berger—a graduate of the Harvard Business School and a moderately rich man—in New York, where the couple lived until 1977. In that year they moved to Dare County, North Carolina. Sometime during the 1970's Mr. Berger inherited about $1.5 million, primarily in the form of com-mercial real estate in New York. Mr. Berger was actively engaged in the real estate development business in North Carolina and other states, and in 1984 his annual income was approximately $170,000.

In 1980, Mr. and Mrs. Berger bought a second house in Norfolk, Virginia, so that Mrs. Berger could live there while the couple's three children attended Virginia private schools. Mrs. Berger spent most of her time with the children in Virginia, but returned to North Carolina on weekends, during vacations, and in summer.

In October 1981 Mrs. Berger filed for divorce in the Circuit Court of the City of Norfolk on grounds of abandonment. At that point Mr. and Mrs. Berger began a five-year trip through the land of chaos that is American law.

Mrs. Berger's Virginia divorce complaint asked for alimony, child support, custody of the children, and a lump sum settlement. However, because Mr. Berger was a resident of North Carolina, the Virginia court ruled that it could award only a divorce and custody to Mrs. Berger—alas, no cigar. For money, the Virginia court ruled, Mrs. Berger had to go to North Carolina where her husband lived—or so everyone thought.

In August 1982 Mrs. Berger filed for divorce in Dare County, North Carolina, and personally served her husband with process in that state. But in the meantime Mr. Berger moved to West Virginia, probably because at that time North Carolina allowed an "equitable distribution of marital property" upon divorce, while West Virginia did not. Thus it was of some moment to Mrs. Berger whether the North Carolina court would have jurisdiction. Mrs. Berger convinced a North Carolina judge that Mr. Berger was a North Carolina resident at the time she filed for divorce and got the North Carolina court to order Mr. Berger to give her about $6,000 a month temporary alimony and child support. By then, however, Mr. Berger had retreated to West Virginia and refused to pay. Mrs. Berger persuaded the North Carolina trial court to take Mr. Berger's property into receivership and hold it hostage for the payment of the court's award, but, to Mrs. Berger's chagrin, most of Mr. Berger's valuable property was outside of North Carolina.

This interstate fiasco came to a climax in July 1983 when Mr. Berger filed for divorce in the Circuit Court of Kanawha County, West Virginia, and served Mrs. Berger with process by publication. All Mr. Berger wanted was a divorce—he already had the money. So Mrs. Berger had no choice but to come to West Virginia to defend her rights in the West Virginia courts. She made a motion to dismiss Mr. Berger's divorce action on the grounds that there was already a divorce proceeding pending in North Carolina, but the West Virginia circuit court agreed with Mr. Berger that the North Carolina court did not have jurisdiction under North Carolina law to grant the parties a divorce because as of 1985 *neither* Mr. nor Mrs. Berger was a resident of North Carolina. Therefore, the West Virginia circuit court decided to go forward with the divorce under West Virginia law, although Mrs. Berger may not have even known that there *was* a *West* Virginia before she was sued there.

Mrs. Berger hired lawyers in West Virginia and went through a trial. Fortunately for her, West Virginia had just changed its divorce law to allow equitable distribution of marital property, so Mrs. Berger received $167,000 in a lump sum distribution plus about $3,000 a month in alimony and child support. But Mrs. Berger was outraged; Mr. Berger paid her instantly and she accepted his check under protest. Mrs. Berger then appealed to the West Virginia Supreme Court of Appeals. In June 1986 the West Virginia Supreme Court of Appeals reversed the West Virginia trial court and sent the whole thing back to North Carolina on the grounds that it was for the North Carolina courts to determine in the first instance whether Mr. Berger had been a resident of North Carolina at the time the North Carolina divorce complaint was filed.

For our purposes here, it should be noted that in a period of roughly five years neither Mr. Berger nor Mrs. Berger achieved anything, although everyone's combined lawyers' fees were probably $30,000. Had Mrs. Berger succeeded in North Carolina, she would have gotten a handsome award; and, had Mr. Berger's ruse of flight to West Virginia worked, he would have gotten out of his marriage fairly cheaply. But as a direct result of our uncommon law, after five years and $30,000 in legal fees, nobody got anything from any court except vexatious litigation and a promise of much more to come.

Several months after the West Virginia Supreme Court of Appeals handed down its decision, Mr. and Mrs. Berger settled the whole matter, obviously recognizing that the courts were hell-bent on sentencing them to death by due process. They were smart, but not all cases can be settled. When we turn to litigation between corporate giants like Texaco and Pennzoil, for whom legal fees are no consideration, we can find cases so complex because of interjurisdictional problems that they support entire law firms for two generations.

Lack of coordination among jurisdictions in the United States simply exacerbates what is, perhaps, the most intractable problem in any sophisticated legal system—namely, the lack of firm rules. There is, however, an irony to the firm rule problem: in general, primitive law systems are characterized by hard-and-fast rules, while advanced law systems are characterized by flexibility. The world's two great secular law systems—namely, Roman law (on which today's European civil law is based) and English common law (on which today's English and American law is based) are systems of principles rather than systems of rules. The difference between a system of principles and a system of rules is like the difference between an alphabetic script and a system of ideographs such as the Chinese.[5] Both Roman lawyers and common lawyers succeeded in designing comprehensive and infinitely adaptable legal systems because they could manipulate abstractions on a scale previously unknown. Furthermore, both Roman and common lawyers were willing to reject the logic of their own constructions when that logic conflicted with the demands of convenience.

But flexibility in a legal system is like belladonna in a sick patient's pharmaceutical regimen. The trick is to prescribe exactly the right amount. The reason the Texas Court of Appeals has not been impeached for outright corruption because of its opinion in *Texaco* is that applicable legal principles are so broad that they can be manipulated to appear to favor Pennzoil. When too much flexibility creeps into a legal system, it ceases to be a legal system at all, because no one can predict the nature or application of rules in advance. In primitive societies the law is fairly clear because society is comparatively simple. People are expected not to kill, maim, rape, or rob one another, and when a crime occurs the community coalesces to apply a sanction through the village chief, village council, or even a local judge.

The same simple process exists in the civil law of primitive societies where disputes usually involve land tenure, as well as contracts centering in agricultural production. Violations of land agreements and breaches of contracts are condemned by the community—there is a consensus about how people should treat one another. Yet part of the reason for the consensus in primitive societies about what the law is and how it should be applied results from an even distribution of wealth. When people are more or less equal—when opportunities are dependent upon industry—a simple code of conduct is also a just code of conduct. But as society

5. This observation was first made by Rudolph von Jhering in his monumental nineteenth-century study of Roman law, *Geist des romischen Rechts* (*Spirit of Roman Law*), 1st ed. (1852–65), which, regretfully, has never been translated into English, although there is a French translation by O. de Meulenaere.

becomes more complex, political cleavages develop that must be accommodated in the legal structure. Usually at the heart of these political cleavages is the unequal distribution of wealth. Once gross wealth inequalities enter the picture, consensus on the fairness of the rules evaporates. This, in fact, is one of the central problems that haunts us whenever we try to modify existing product liability law.

When all litigants live, vote, hire workers, and pay taxes in the same jurisdiction, the tension between firm rules and necessary flexibility can be kept within reasonable bounds. Thus if Texaco had been a real, operating Texas company instead of a New York company, it would almost certainly have received different treatment at the hands of the Texas courts. But when each state's system is in the business of redistributing wealth from out-of-state defendants to in-state plaintiffs, as in the *Texaco* case, the caprice of an infinitely flexible set of principles becomes hazardous to our commercial health. In-state defendants are often protected by local juries, but out-of-state defendants have nothing to rely upon but a firm set of legal rules. This, in fact, is the entire crux of the product liability problem. The *Texaco* case is a grandiose example of intentional home cooking; while ordinary product liability cases are also sometimes examples of intentional home cooking, usually they are examples of unintentional home cooking that emerges naturally from the structure of our system. To change the metaphor, our judicial system allows the home team to hire all the umpires in matches with the visitors. The fact that typically a product liability suit is brought by an in-state plaintiff against an out-of-state defendant allows the courts to craft the legal rules themselves in product liability in such a way that the defendant always loses.

In our current system, how does an out-of-state manufacturer defend against a suit for alleged injury from an "ultra-hazardous" product it has manufactured? According to the *Restatement of Torts* (a compendium and commentary on current tort law published by the American Law Institute, and often cited as authority by courts around the country), liability for an ultra-hazardous product or activity depends upon: (1) the riskiness of the activity; (2) whether the product is in common usage; (3) whether reasonable precautions could have avoided the risk; (4) whether risk is inherent; and (5) whether the cost of prevention exceeds the social benefits. These are infinitely flexible standards that instruct no one's understanding in advance of whether a product is ultra-hazardous, or what actions must be taken to avoid liability. Furthermore, and more to the point for our purposes here, it is inevitable that fuzzy standards like these will be applied arbitrarily against out-of-state defendants.

The problems of lack of uniformity, lack of predictability, and lack of consistency are becoming acute because there is an ongoing shift in the center of political power—it is moving away from legislatures, executives, and administrative agencies in the direction of the courts.[6] Although it is easier to mobilize the courts to take action against social problems than it is to mobilize legislatures or executives, courts have more limited tools with which to work than do other branches of government. In my experience, the theory on which activist judges usually operate is that a poor judge-made solution to a problem is better than no solution at all.

Product liability law is a superb example of the inefficiency of local state-court-designed solutions to social problems. For every dollar received by the victims of product-related accidents, roughly three to five dollars go to lawyers and administrators, depending on the type of case. The Social Security Administration, on the other hand, administers a nationwide system of disability insurance for approximately four cents on each dollar paid to beneficiaries.[7] First-party insurance, then, is a cheaper, more efficient way to protect everyone from society's unavoidable risks than tort liability, but mandating a nationwide, first-party insurance system was never an option open to courts. And, to be fair about the matter, neither Congress nor state legislatures would ever have given us comprehensive social insurance because the rich don't want to pay for the poor. Unelected judges can redistribute wealth, albeit inefficiently, better than elected legislators, and the recipients of

6. Parliamentary democracy is slow, cumbersome, expensive, and thoroughly corrupt. When people feel that they have urgent problems that the inertia-prone or corrupt machinery of elected government cannot or will not solve, they look for ways both to shortcut and short-circuit the standard government process. The courts have the ability to do both, and so they are widely used; the more they are used, the more we get used to them, and the stronger they become.

7. My own private disability insurance policy for $18,000 a year of lifetime, tax-free benefits, should I become disabled, has cost me only $500 a year since 1969.

this redistributed wealth become a powerful political lobby supporting the power of courts.[8]

Compared to Congress or a state legislature, any court—including the U.S. Supreme Court—has primitive tools for fixing some (but not all) social breakdowns. Many of our truly troublesome product liability issues are directly related to the fact that courts *want* to solve the social problem of unavoidable risks in an increasingly dangerous society, but have limited tools for doing so. Often, when a court takes hold of a social problem, the exercise is similar to what happens when a child takes hold of a balloon full of water: grabbing the balloon at one place simply causes it to bulge someplace else. Judicial solutions to urgent social problems are frequently based on political and sociological theories whose cogency and coherence depend on long chains of assumptions and inferences joined by weak or nonexistent links.[9]

The structural rigidities and imperfections of other branches of government provide some very good reasons why we will need to contend with court solutions to social problems for the foreseeable future, inefficient and often ill-conceived though such solutions may be.[10] But the problem of government by judiciary is

8. In this regard it is interesting to note one other expanding function of federal courts—namely, appeals from denials of federal social security benefits. As the acceptable national rate of unemployment has risen from about 4 percent in the 1970's to 7 percent in the 1980's, we have increasingly come to depend on disability insurance to perform the functions of long-term unemployment insurance. The Reagan administration has attempted to narrow disability eligibility, but the federal courts have resisted these efforts. In my estimation, this is a terribly important (but not particularly complicated) function of the federal courts. The background, experience, and humanitarian impulses of federal judges make them a necessary counterweight to inflexible bureaucrats. Were it not for social security insurance, our national problem of homelessness would be much more acute than it now is, and our official unemployment rate would also be much higher. See D. Stone, *The Disabled State* (Philadelphia: Temple University Press, 1984).

9. For example, in the last eight years there have been numerous suits against school systems because students have failed to learn. Judges, like most progressive people, favor effective, high quality, public education, yet judges can't take over the schools or appropriate the money to run them. The temptation to impose liability on teachers for a student's poor learning proceeds from the belief that liability will force teachers to do a better job. In my experience it doesn't work that way, but the theory seems logical enough at first glance.

10. I have addressed another entire book to this particular subject. See *How Courts Govern America* (New Haven: Yale University Press, 1981).

made much worse than it need be by lack of a unified system of common law on interstate matters. A state court, for example, is not capable of deciding the appropriate trade-off between the value of cheap mass inoculations for such diseases as polio, and the rights of individuals unlucky enough to contract the disease from the vaccine. If, as a state court judge, I rule that a person contracting polio from the Sabin vaccine is entitled only to net economic losses—i.e., uninsured medical expenses, lost income, and special life support equipment—and I do so to encourage universal vaccination, I have no assurance that judges in California or Massachusetts won't put vaccine manufacturers out of business or drive up the price of vaccine by adopting a far more generous rule for their own local plaintiffs, one that allows open-ended awards for pain and suffering. Yet the Supreme Court of the United States can limit vaccine manufacturers' liability to net economic loss, and in so doing know that, although a few unlucky victims won't receive compensation for pain and suffering, scores of millions of young children will continue to be protected from dread diseases because the vaccines will remain both cheap and readily available.

In this last regard it should be remembered that just thirty-five years ago polio afflicted more than 57,000 Americans. Only four cases were reported in 1984. No less dramatic is the decline of whooping cough, brought about by the pertussis component of the DPT vaccine. The incidence of pertussis in the United States dropped from more than 265,000 cases and 7,500 deaths in 1934 to fewer than 2,000 cases and only four deaths in 1982. As the incidence of preventable diseases declines, however, the incentive to be vaccinated against such diseases also declines, particularly among the poor and uneducated. Administered once or only a few times in a recipient's lifetime, vaccines are low-margin products. They generate only slight profits and possible huge losses due to damage awards, so they represent an unacceptable risk to manufacturers. As manufacturers withdraw from the vaccine business, those remaining will be able to raise prices, which in turn will discourage immunization in low-income families unless the cost is borne by public authorities.[11]

11. Recent congressional legislation has taken a promising, although not wholly adequate, step in the direction of solving this problem. H.R. 5186, signed into law by President Reagan on 14 November 1986, created a no-fault compen-

A tightening-up of the perimeters within which the fifty-three separate American court systems have full rein to be eccentric will not solve most of the problems that business faces in court because there are practical limits to the federal courts' ability to *enforce* uniformity. These limits dictate that a national common law must focus on interstate transactions, which leaves in the hands of local courts such questions as the liability of local employers for discharging employees in an allegedly unlawful manner, or the liability of local ski resorts for accidents occurring on their slopes. But with regard to interstate questions like the liability of national vaccine manufacturers, a national common law should establish clear, bright-line standards that will reduce many of our current judicial hazards.

The increasing complexity and uncertainty of today's decisional law is directly related to a geometrically expanding judicial bureaucracy at both state and federal levels. Consequently, part of the value of national law is that it can limit the number of permutations and combinations of existing principles and also control the creation of new principles. In the main, this was the exact theory upon which the original, highly successful common law was based. In the nineteenth century, for example, the judging business was a cottage industry in which political good ol' boys (who became judges for the job's prestige and leisure) wrote their own opinions out in longhand. Many of the lawyers of that era were trained in law office apprenticeships, and those who went to law school attended institutions where the emphasis was on

---

sation fund under which payments will be made to the families of persons who suffer injuries or death as a result of receiving vaccines generally required by state law. Under the new law, persons seeking redress for vaccine-related injuries or death are required initially to file a petition for compensation through the no-fault fund in federal district court. A person establishing a vaccine-related injury or death may be awarded medical expenses, death benefits, lost earnings, and attorneys' fees. Awards for pain and suffering are limited to $250,000, and punitive damages are not allowed. In case of death, a lump sum of $250,000 is awarded.

However, the homogenizing effect of this legislation is vitiated by sections of the law permitting a plaintiff who is unhappy with his award under the fund to reject the award and sue the manufacturer in state or federal court. These sections do establish *some* uniform standards concerning the manufacturer's *liability*, but they place no limits on the kind or amount of compensatory and punitive damages that may be awarded. Thus, until Congress or the federal courts step in to seal off this escape hatch, the heterogeneity of state law will continue to plague our efforts to achieve good public health through universal vaccination.

quite pedestrian practitioner skills. Both judges and lawyers argued primarily by assertion, cutting and pasting well-known precedents to achieve what appeared to them to be reasonable results. But a major institutional rearrangement occurred with the litigation explosion of the 1960's that corresponded to the shift in political power in the direction of the courts: Between 1960 (the eve of the explosion) and 1983, civil case filings in the federal courts alone increased from 51,063 to 241,159.[12]

But although the federal caseload increased by nearly fivefold in twenty-three years, the number of federal judges barely doubled. The same phenomenon occurred in varying degrees in the state courts. The caseload problem was solved by building a bureaucracy whose increasing presence and significance are evidenced by the fact that during the same period that available judge time per case was rapidly decreasing, the length and complexity of judicial opinions was steadily increasing. For example, in 1894 the average justice of the U.S. Supreme Court wrote 23 opinions and produced a total of 60,000 published words a year. In 1983, the average Supreme Court justice wrote 39 opinions and produced 146,000 published words a year. Between 1960 and 1983 the average number of words in published U.S. Court of Appeals opinions increased from 2,774 to 4,023.[13] Of course, the reason that courts can decide many more cases per judge than they did twenty-five years ago, and, at the same time, write twice as much verbiage in each case, is that judges no longer write their own opinions.

Appellate judges have been transformed from articulators of their own reasoning to supervisors of opinion-drafting law clerks. Judges are still political good ol' boys, and they still decide cases on political principles, but because they are not any more enamored of work than the average posthole digger, they turn the drudgery of opinion writing over to a host of young, well-trained, academically inclined recent law school graduates. When a judge decides a case he can now simply instruct his clerk to "put something together" to justify the result. If the opinion seems reasonable when it comes across the judge's desk, it gets published.

Law clerks, however, don't think like old common-law judges;

12. See R. A. Posner, *The Federal Courts* (Cambridge, Mass.: Harvard University Press, 1985), pp. 59–65.

13. *Ibid.*, p. 114.

they think like the law professors they have just spent three years trying to impress. Many of the best law clerks have recently come from America's prestigious law schools, where their heads have been filled with complex and convoluted legal theories. The problem is that, in the practical world that judicial opinions are supposed to instruct, the most valuable attribute is simplicity and clarity. But in academia, unhappily, the emphasis is always on obscurity, brilliance, and novelty.

Prestigious law reviews (on which academics depend for career advancement) do not publish articles extolling the virtues of clear, simple, existing rules, like the one requiring that there be an offer and acceptance to form a contract. It is the business of academic law to criticize the current legal structure and to suggest whole new systems for processing litigation. In many areas of law, this is like suggesting that automobiles be built with seven wheels, or that tractor trailers be mounted on roller skates, but that doesn't make the problem any less severe.

I have already discussed the flexible and manipulable test set forth in the *Restatement of Torts* for determining liability for ultrahazardous products and activities. Another area into which the *Restatement* drafters have introduced unpredictability is "conflicts of law." "Conflicts of law" is the body of law that instructs a court regarding which state's law shall be applied to a case when more than one state has some contact with the dispute. Conflicts doctrine is designed to answer questions like, "If a West Virginia resident and an Ohio resident collide with a Missouri resident on an Indiana highway, which state's liability rules apply to the suit of the Ohio passenger against the West Virginia driver?"

The traditional rule governing such cases was that the law of the state where the injury occurred would apply. But by the 1960's judges and legal commentators were growing increasingly dissatisfied with the substantive results rendered by application of the traditional rule. In response, the American Law Institute drafted the *Restatement (Second) of Conflicts of Law,* which sets forth the following criteria as pertinent to a choice of law in a personal injury case: (1) the place where the injury occurred; (2) the place where the conduct causing the injury occurred; (3) the domicile, residence, nationality, place of incorporation, and place of business of the parties; (4) the place where the relationship, if any, between the parties, is centered; (5) the needs of the interstate and international systems; (6) the relevant policies of the forum; (7) the rele-

vant policies of other interested states, and the relative interest of
those states in the determination of the particular issue; (8) the
protection of justified expectations; (9) the basic policies underlying the particular field of law; (10) certainty, predictability, and
uniformity of results; and (11) ease in the determination and application of the law to be applied.

This approach to questions involving conflicts of law has now
been adopted by nearly half of the states. The result of its adoption has been the creation of so much legal entropy that it is arguably the single most significant contributor to the acceleration of
the heat death of the universe. And wafting from this heap of legal
chaos is the unmistakable aroma of home cooking. One court has
described the *Restatement* approach as "not a rule, but a method
of analysis that permitted dissection of the jural bundle constitut-
ing a tort and its environment."[14] But an examination of the cases
indicates that the *Restatement* approach is in fact a method of
avoiding the application of laws of other states that would protect
insurance companies from injured plaintiffs.

The confusion engendered by the *Restatement* approach is nicely
illustrated in two cases decided by the New York courts. In *Babcock
v. Jackson,* a guest passenger in an automobile sued her host in New
York for injuries caused by the host's negligence while driving in
Ontario. Under New York law, the guest could recover for injuries
caused by the host's lack of ordinary care, but the Ontario guest
statute barred such a recovery. The New York court permitted the
guest to recover in spite of the fact that the injuries occurred in
Ontario. The court held that New York had the "dominant contacts" with the dispute, because the parties lived in New York and
were traveling in a car registered and regularly garaged in New
York. The only connection Ontario had with the dispute, the court
noted, was that the accident happened to take place there.

Kell v. Henderson, another New York decision, also presented a
case in which a guest sued a host for injuries sustained in an automobile collision. In this case, however, the guest was from Ontario,
the host was from Ontario, the car was registered and regularly
garaged in Ontario, and the trip was to begin and end in Ontario.
New York's only connection with the dispute was that the accident
happened to take place there. The New York court nevertheless
held, while putatively following *Babcock,* that New York law rather

14. *Conklin v. Horner,* 38 Wis.2d 468, 473, 157 N.W.2d 579, 581 (1968).

than Ontario law applied. It was perhaps recognition of just such gross disparities in result that prompted the Court of Appeals of New York to remark, in a towering achievement in the art of understatement, "candor requires the admission that our past decisions have lacked a precise consistency."[15]

Whenever I find state courts establishing balancing tests with no well-defined criteria—like the *Restatement* rules on ultra-hazardous products and conflicts of law—or see them constructing new theories of liability, I feel the same way that I do when my six-year-old son wants to play with my loaded twelve-gauge shotgun. It's not that he will necessarily blow my head off, it's just that the smart money doesn't bet against that outcome.

When the tools of academic law are in the hands of the truly brilliant they are likely to be used skillfully; when they are placed in the hands of second-rate epigones, however, the results can be surprisingly perverse. For example, some state courts have figured out theories under which plaintiffs can sue manufacturers from whom they never bought a product, merely because those manufacturers are part of an industry that has sold defective products.

A national common law should help restore a better balance between clear rules and flexibility because, for entirely practical reasons, there can be no room at the national level for soft standards. When nine judges on an overworked court that decides only 150 cases a year try to guide the day-to-day decisions of thousands of magistrates, trial judges, and appellate judges, only clear, definite rules can be used. Federal control of the state courts depends upon voluntary and enthusiastic compliance by state judges with the rules of the U.S. Supreme Court.[16] However, before state courts can do what the federal courts tell them to do, the rules must be clear.

In the *Pennzoil v. Texaco* case, for example, the U.S. Supreme Court reversed the federal appeals court judgment on the grounds that Texas has an "open court" provision in its state constitution, and that, if Texaco had gone to the Texas courts with its claim that the Texas bond statute violated its federal rights to due process, the Texas courts would probably have given it relief. But this rul-

15. *Miller v. Miller,* 22 N.Y.2d 12, 237 N.E.2d 877, 879 (1968).
16. I have been a judge of West Virginia's highest court for over fifteen years, and in that period our court has been reversed only twice by the U.S. Supreme Court. Both cases involved complicated interstate tax issues, and in both cases the Supreme Court promulgated new standards.

ing missed a great opportunity: problems like Texaco's would be solved forever if the Supreme Court had simply said that due process requires a right to appeal, and that unreasonable bond statutes simply can't be enforced against losing defendants if complying with them would effectively foreclose appeal rights.

There are three examples of federal court control of state courts demonstrating the proposition that national uniformity requires bright-line rules understandable by even the most mediocre lawyer or judge. The first example concerns the procedural aspects of the criminal law—such things as, when a confession is valid, what is required to search a person's house, and when a lawyer must be appointed for a defendant at state expense. Half of the cases in state courts are criminal cases, and the sheer volume of criminal cases guarantees that occasionally there will be questions that do not fall squarely within any previous Supreme Court ruling. But for the hundreds of thousands of prosecutions each year that are settled by plea bargains or by quick trial court decisions, the rules are very clear.

The second example involves libel and slander cases against the media, where the Supreme Court has said that you can't get a judgment against a media defendant unless you can prove that: (1) the material published was false; (2) the defendant knew that it was false at the time of publication, or behaved with reckless disregard of the truth; and, (3) the material was intentionally published to injure the plaintiff. By the standards of today's tort law, those are extremely clear-cut, bright-line rules.

The third example involves state taxation of interstate commerce, where the Supreme Court has said that a state can't discriminate against interstate commerce by singling out imports or exports for special taxes, and that when taxing the income or personal property of an interstate business, states must apply apportionment formulae that would yield fair taxes if applied by every other state. There are a few other wrinkles, but for tax specialists the rules are pretty simple.

Given the other demands on federal courts, it is inevitable that they will limit any unification initiative to serious interstate problems. However, the federal courts not only have immense power, they also have immense prestige. Consequently, the rules that the federal courts craft for interstate problems are also likely to be applied by the state courts to local problems, simply because Supreme Court decisions are usually good precedent—that is to say, they present well-thought-out, intelligent approaches to recurring problems.

We can end this general discussion with one concrete example. State courts currently apply something known as the "collateral source rule," in product liability cases. Under the "collateral source rule," the defendant is not given credit toward its damages for workers' compensation or for first-party insurance when these are available to the plaintiff. As we will see later, the reason for this is to terrify defendants into settling out-of-court. But one bright-line rule that the federal courts could make in interstate product liability cases is that if the defendant agrees to pay quickly for *net* economic losses and reasonable attorneys' fees, then money received by the plaintiff from collateral sources such as workers' compensation and employer medical insurance is a credit against the defendants' damages. Given that what the system wants is the quick, fair compensation of injured victims, and not a Las Vegas roulette game, that basic rule (with inevitable refinements) is an improvement over the current system.

But although the federal courts could mandate such a rule for interstate suits, the federal courts don't have the manpower (or, arguably, the authority) to enforce it in other contexts. Yet the rule is still likely to be adopted by state courts for intrastate matters. One reason such a rule has not *already* been adopted for intrastate matters is that it would reduce the ability of state courts to redistribute wealth from out-of-state defendants to in-state plaintiffs. Once, however, the rule is forced on state courts for interstate matters, there is little incentive for state courts to retain the more severe rule for their own local defendants.

Before old law will be changed or new law created there must be a demonstrated need. What I am trying to do is not to explore exhaustively the possible permutations of arcane legal principles, but simply demonstrate the need for, and benefits from, a system of uniform, federally imposed standards on interstate civil matters, particularly in product liability cases. Certainly there are numerous ways in which existing principles can be legitimately manipulated to yield the result. The most obvious fulcrum for the U.S. Supreme Court's lawmaking lever in these matters is the Constitution's commerce clause, but the Fourteenth Amendment's due process and equal protection clauses are also vessels sufficiently empty that national standards law can be poured into them. It is a waste of time to set out any particular, concrete theory because that theory would then sit idly waiting for a set of facts tailored to the theory.

From a practical point of view, the first step in the process of establishing national standards is not a new legal theory, but rather professional acceptance of the legitimacy of a national common law. Once enough people say, "That's a good idea!" all that remains is to offer concrete opportunities to implement the idea in the context of pending cases. Lawyers throughout America have cases involving clients for whom the lawyer's running meter is of no consequence, and many of these cases present opportunities to argue for the establishment of a national standard in some particular area. If during every term of the U.S. Supreme Court a hundred lawyers bring cases presenting opportunities for law unification, the Supreme Court will eventually let one or two cases in and begin the ten-year process of national common-law development. In this regard I am reminded of India's Nehru who, after successfully orchestrating independence for more than 400 million people, frankly admitted to Lord Mountbatten that he hadn't the faintest idea how to run the country. Starting revolutions is the work of politicians; finishing them is the work of lawyers.

Chapter 3

The Competitive Race
to the Bottom

The suggestion that the federal courts should play a larger role in American law will be received initially by business with little enthusiasm. This is a perfectly understandable reaction because the most vocal supporters of an expanding federal judiciary over the last thirty years have been environmentalists, minorities, trial lawyers, and academics—all the folks, in other words, who are the adversaries of business. But in areas like product liability it hardly seems possible that new law generated by the federal courts could be worse than the law that business currently lives under in the local state courts. In many areas of the law, therefore, urging that the federal courts impose unifying national rules involves exclusively an upside risk for business. Already in some areas, like the duplication of punitive damages when there are numerous state court lawsuits but only one wrongful act, it is the business lawyers who are urging an expanded role for federal courts.

There are two distinct aspects to federal court unification of the law on business-related matters. The first aspect involves the extent of business's liability under new, national rules, but the second and more important aspect involves the value of uniformity *per se.* Business, obviously, would have unreserved enthusiasm for law unification if it thought that for *political* reasons (such as domination of the federal judiciary by conservatives) the new rules would be less oriented to wealth redistribution than the current hodgepodge of state rules. Such a result, however, is extremely unlikely. In some areas of the law, like the emerging tort of "unlawful discharge," it is more likely that any national rule on employment tenure in private enterprise would actually be *less* favorable to business than state law is today. In government personnel firings, for example (an area currently covered under an expansive interpretation of the federal civil rights act), the federal courts have not been reluctant to craft law extremely unfavorable to government employers. Furthermore, this pro-employee law was produced by the Republican-appointed Burger court.

However, the value of the second aspect of uniformity—namely, uniformity *per se*—has nothing whatsoever to do with the competence, social outlook, or political philosophies of federal judges *vis-à-vis* state judges. Rather, uniformity *per se* has to do exclusively with the sociology of different judicial decision-making *structures*. The political factors that currently affect judicial decisions, such as the philosophies and backgrounds of individual judges, will be about the same in a new, unified system as they are in the current chaotic system. But in a new, unified system the sociological climate in which broad political decisions are made will change substantially for the better. All of this probably sounds needlessly academic, but the bottom line is that now the *structure* of the American judicial system—all liberal or conservative politics aside—makes it impossible for judges to take into consideration national economic growth goals, even if they wanted to do so.

If, for example, you ask the average liberal judge simply whether he would like to redistribute some wealth from General Motors to a local resident who was severely injured in a car crash, the judge will probably answer "yes." But if you ask the same judge to make a choice between high local employment in General Motors' plants on the one hand, and redistribution of General Motors' wealth to injured accident victims on the other, the same judge is likely to favor high employment over simple wealth redistribution. Indeed, such a response is entirely predictable, because a high rate of employment—particularly in high-wage jobs—tends to cure numerous social problems at once. Easy access to employment provides upward mobility to the culturally disadvantaged; slums are evacuated in the wake of rising incomes; and government revenues rise with private employment to allow improved social services. In fact, a snapshot glance at the western world in 1987 indicates that systemic *unemployment* is probably the most serious social problem facing all industrialized, democratic countries.

It implies no inconsistency to predict, then, that a judge will give General Motors' money to an accident victim if the choice is simply between wealth for the victim and wealth for G.M.'s stockholders, but the same judge will not give money to the victim if the choice is between helping victims and sustaining jobs. The judge's political philosophy has not changed at all, but the question he or she is asked has changed, and the changed question forces him or her to balance competing *liberal* goals. Thus, whether the results that business gets in court are favorable or unfavorable depends to some extent on the breadth of the interests that the court must balance. When, therefore, I talk about changing the sociological structure in which judicial decisions are made, I am simply talking about placing ultimate lawmaking authority in the hands of national judges who can balance a larger number of competing considerations. To the U.S. Supreme Court, after all, everything is "local."

Everyone understands that the rich and powerful inspire little affection among most people, and ironically the term "most people" often includes the rich and powerful themselves. Rich and powerful newspaper publishers, for example, devote much of their working time to castigating every other rich and powerful group in America. Even the handsomely paid minions of the rich and powerful feel little devotion to their masters. For example, the *Stanford Law Review* reported in 1985, on the basis of extensive empirical data, that business lawyers are significantly more "liberal" than their business clients. Almost half the business lawyers interviewed (48.2%) disagreed with the statement: "On the whole, rules governing occupational safety and health impose undue burdens on employers." And almost as many business lawyers (46.4%) disagreed with the statement: "Economic profits are by and large justly distributed in the United States today."[1] Therefore, even if business could ring the political chimes and get a host of business-oriented lawyers appointed to the bench, that triumph alone would not necessarily mean new pro-business law. When business lawyers become judges, they often devote the rest of their lives to doing penance for having been business whores when they were young. I have served with some of these black-robed Magdalenes and they can be more irrational than old AFL-CIO head busters.

It is, therefore, not love and affection that protect business generally, but rather necessity. If, indeed, widespread, high-wage em-

1. R. L. Nelson, "Ideology, Practice, and Professional Autonomy: Social Values and Client Relationships in the Large Law Firm," 37 *Stan. L. Rev.* 503.

ployment is the near-universal elixir for social ills, then the only fountain of that elixir is private business. Without productive private enterprise, where most jobs are based on efficiency measured by competitive markets, government employment becomes simply an exercise in taking in one another's washing. Unemployment is even a problem that faces communist countries. Recent liberal reforms in China, for example, are prompted in large measure by that economy's inability to employ all the young persons entering the labor force in the cities along the eastern coast. Although workers can always be employed in rural, subsistence agriculture, young urbanites in Shanghai or Beijing want to stay in their home cities. The unemployment rate is disguised by the tendency of young adults to live at home, unemployed, under the guise of "studying" for the university entrance exams. In fact, these young adults are out of work, but application for a state-guaranteed job would result in exile to some rural backwater. Thus, they all hang around hoping that family connections (*guan shi*) will eventually land them an urban job.

John Rawls, the liberal Harvard philosopher who wrote a whole treatise in the early 1970's in favor of wealth equality, finally conceded that inequalities in wealth must be allowed if they favor "the least favored group."[2] Thus Rawls pointed out that brain surgeons must be allowed to make more money than factory workers to encourage surgeons to undergo arduous training. But, as Rawls so eloquently argues, before the rich and the powerful will be tolerated there must be some correlation between their welfare and the welfare of everyone else. John Rawls, of course, is substantially to the left of most mainstream American liberals, but the fact that even he allows some place for the rich in a perfectly "just" society—based on their contribution to the welfare of others—is a monument to the relevance in lawmaking of considerations of economic growth, aggregate employment, and America's flagging competitive position in international markets.

I am the first to concede that judges are often motivated by knee-jerk, anti-business sentiments. But much of the law that adversely affects business and is contrary to the national interest arises simply because intelligent and well-meaning state and federal judges are not asked, or even allowed, to consider the national

2. J. Rawls, *A Theory of Justice* (Cambridge, Mass.: Harvard University Press, 1971).

economic interest. In fact, if we examine a typical product liability suit in a local state or federal court,[3] we will discover that all of the social dynamics work against taking into consideration any factors concerning national economic policy, and, therefore, everything works against business.

Because of home cooking problems, business defendants almost always attempt to remove state court cases to the more professional federal courts. Federal judges, however, are busy and unenthusiastic about additional work, so the federal courts have established numerous obstacles to federal court diversity jurisdiction. Preëminent among these obstacles is something known as the "full diversity" rule that requires all parties on the defendant's side to be non-residents of the state in which the action was brought. Plaintiffs' lawyers who covet the appetizing prospect of tasty home cooking have become skilled at developing devices to defeat diversity jurisdiction and to keep cases in state courts. The most useful device for this purpose is to find a local, in-state defendant—such as a distributor—to sue in addition to the out-of-state, target defendant. Once the case has progressed sufficiently to establish firm jurisdiction in the state court, the nominal in-state defendant can be dismissed, leaving the out-of-state company with the deep pocket to take the entire hit.

Let us look, then, at who the players in a product liability suit brought in state court are, and where they usually come from. The plaintiff is typically an injured individual who comes from the same vicinity as the judge and jury, and the defendant is typically an out-of-state, publicly held corporation. The jury are local people who come from a wide spectrum of society but are disproportionately retired persons and housewives. The desperately poor tend not to appear on the standard rolls used for jury selec-

---

3. Under current law, if a case is filed in or removed to federal court because of diversity of citizenship, the federal court is obliged to apply the decisional law of the highest state court of the state where the federal court sits. Consequently, local federal judges are not allowed to look to some national standard in adjudicating claims brought under state law, but must look to the law of the state. Furthermore, there is no "national" law of product liability. Most tort causes of action arise under the law of the individual states. Sometimes these causes of action are based on statutes, but more often they are based on the state's decisional law. A federal court sitting in a diversity case, then, will be just as provincial as any state court, although the federal judge may be better trained than his state counterparts and the federal court more efficiently run than the state court across the street.

tion. The upper socio-economic classes are busy and typically use every available device to get excused from jury duty. A judge has a hard time demanding jury service from a surgeon whose time in court may jeopardize the lives of his patients, and it is no easier to demand jury service from a small business owner who cannot be replaced at the factory. Even salesmen will be excused if they can show that they will lose customers by being kept off the road.

Some courts have tried to expand jury selection into the ranks of the poor by taking jurors from the welfare rolls. Other courts have attempted to recruit the rich by shortening the length of jury service. But in most places the courts simply muddle through, missing the really poor and excusing professionals, executives, mothers with young children, and anyone over sixty-five who doesn't want to serve. The unemployed love jury duty because it pays a fee; housewives with grown children often like to serve; people with dull, monotonous, steady jobs to which they can easily return don't complain; and healthy, retired people often find jury duty diverting. Most juries, therefore, are disproportionately composed of these types of people.

Finally we come to the state court judge. In twenty-two states, he or she is elected by the voters for a set term—typically six years. In some states judges are appointed by the governor until retirement age; in others they are elected by the legislature; and in a number of states judges are appointed initially by the governor but must run regularly in retention elections where the only question asked is: "Should Judge Wossname be retained?" One aspect of the *Pennzoil v. Texaco* case which caused Texaco's lawyers to scream like stuck pigs was that the lead counsel on Pennzoil's side contributed $10,000 to the trial judge's election during the case. In Texas all judges are elected on a partisan ballot.

At least in the states where judges are directly elected by popular vote, like Texas or West Virignia, it should be obvious that the in-state local plaintiff, his witnesses, and his friends, can all vote for the judge, while the out-of-state defendant can't even be relied upon to send a campaign contribution. This is one reason that defendants flee to federal court whenever possible. I can vouch from personal experience that the campaign contribution problem is extremely acute and almost impossible to handle. Elected judges must have campaign money, and its only available source is lawyers or the clients whom the lawyers can strong-arm. In West Virginia we have attempted to reduce the problem by discouraging large contributions, so that all lawyers can participate on a reasonable basis. We would have held in the *Pennzoil v. Texaco* case that $10,000 was too much to contribute, and would have disqualified the judge. The Texas Court of Appeals, however, pointed out explicitly that judges need money and the only place to get it is from lawyers. That's like saying in a child sexual abuse case that if a girl's not good enough for her kin, who is she good enough for? But where do you draw the line? Quite frankly we don't know, but the general rule probably should be that the contribution is too much if it exceeds the average judge's "price," a rule that Abraham Lincoln allegedly articulated once when he kicked a lobbyist out of his office because the offered bribe came too close to his own "price." Ten thousand dollars will buy a lawyer a lot of goodwill, and few lawyers can afford such a contribution. It's just too much.

However, the problem of local plaintiffs, judges, and juries on the one hand *versus* out-of-state corporations on the other is not just the kind of home cooking bias pure and simple that we see in *Texaco*. The far more intractable problem is that all of the arguments that can be made in favor of the plaintiff can be presented to the jury and easily understood by them, while the arguments that can be made on behalf of the business defendant usually go to issues of national economic policy that cannot be presented in a coherent fashion in the trial of the case.[4]

Let us, for example, assume that an injury arose from a defective machine tool manufactured in Springfield, Vermont, twenty years ago. If the case is tried in California the only questions that the jury must answer are: (1) did the product have a design defect? (2) did the design defect cause the injury? (3) did the plaintiff misuse the product or help cause the injury? and, (4) how much are the plaintiff's damages? But there are a lot of other issues that relate to national employment and economic growth goals that a defendant could raise, but that are currently of no political interest to a California trial or appellate court.

In the case of the Vermont manufacturer one could rightfully ask whether there was any product liability law at the time the machine was manufactured that would have inspired the manufacturer to insure. If the manufacturer had no reasonable notice that it could be held liable for a defective product, and thus had no

---

4. I have discussed this problem in detail in *Judicial Jeopardy: When Business Collides with the Courts* (Reading, Mass.: Addison-Wesley, 1986), chapters 6 and 7.

insurance, who will now pay the judgment? If yesterday's judgments must be paid from today's revenues, will this particular company and other small companies be put out of business, and if so, how many jobs will be lost? Are plaintiffs as a class better off in this type of case if we craft special rules of damages that limit pain and suffering awards, but allow some recovery to defray disability costs? Such special rules would have the effect of keeping the company in business to pay something to the next plaintiff. But the next plaintiff will not come from California, so his fate is of no concern to the California courts.

Often, as in the case of Johns Manville (asbestos litigation) or A. H. Robins (Dalkon Shield birth-control-device litigation) these types of questions are answered by the federal bankruptcy courts after numerous judgments have been entered against the company in either state or federal trial courts. This is particularly the pattern when it becomes obvious that the company has done something that will continue to result in liability in the future as new plaintiffs discover their injuries or become aware of their right to sue. When the aggregate of potential future claims is such that the company will not be able to pay them as they mature, the company declares bankruptcy. This lets the bankruptcy court establish a plan under which the company can continue in business by establishing a fund to pay present and future claims on some basis that allows the equitable division of whatever limited resources are available. These plans, however, are very difficult to devise, and even more difficult to get accepted. In the case of Manville, it was expected by most people who watch that company, including stock market professionals, that an acceptable plan would be devised and accepted by the end of 1986. But by the end of 1987 the bankruptcy litigation was still spinning itself out, with the untoward result that Manville continued to mark time, with no opportunity to invest new capital or otherwise revive a company that should again be a strong national and international industry leader. Had these problems been more quickly resolved, Manville would probably have employed several thousand additional workers, either directly or indirectly, and would once again be an aggressive American competitor in world markets.

The types of questions I have just raised go well beyond the specific facts of any particular lawsuit. Political scientists call such considerations "legislative facts," and they are the type of considerations that should affect the overall policy of the decisional law. Occasionally, appellate courts discuss legislative facts explicitly in their published opinions; more often, the legislative facts that influence their decisions remain in the background, while the foreground is dominated by analyses of case law written in the law's peculiar jargon by young clerks.

In fact, appellate courts take *relevant* legislative facts into consideration all the time. Sometimes they are presented to the court by the parties, either through expert testimony, or through citation to published research; however, more often than not judges conjure up the legislative facts from their own limited experience. Furthermore, for a legislative fact to be "relevant" to the judge's own internal decision-making process, it must have something to do with the constituency that the judge is appointed or elected to serve. Obviously, then, aggregate employment in Vermont is not a legislative fact of any relevance to a judge sitting in California. And, unfortunately, such a consideration becomes relevant to a federal bankruptcy court only to the extent that continuing employment expands the pool of resources available to pay unsecured creditors. If the creditors get more by closing the company down and selling off the assets, then that is what will occur.

Unfortunately for business, the fireside equities in most lawsuits are distinctly at odds with considerations of national economic policy. By "fireside equities" I mean simply our gut feelings about who ought to win lawsuits. When a person has been seriously injured by a large industrial machine our sympathies are with him and not with some distant, anonymous company in Springfield, Vermont. The company can't even introduce competing evidence concerning how many people it employs and whether it will be bankrupted by a judgment in an effort to give some balance to fireside considerations.

Kevin Hyde, my roommate in law school, was a conservative engineer from Notre Dame who is now a patent lawyer. One of the things that Kevin used to look for in the court opinions that we were studying was something he called the "Pandora's box" argument. Kevin's rule was that whenever a judge said that acceding to a particular argument made by a plaintiff would "open up Pandora's box," about four pages further on in the opinion some poor, crippled old woman would end up being bankrupted and lose her life's savings. Throughout my fifteen years as a judge I have often thought about Kevin's observation that dwelling too much on any "Pandora's box" implications in a case may lead to needlessly heartless results.

Perhaps the essence of the judicial function, when we are deciding cases between individuals in desperate straits and anonymous, bloodless corporate giants, is striking some balance between the demands of equity (which often means charity) and considerations of economic policy. That choice is always difficult and never permanent. Nonetheless, it is possible at certain points in the system to improve things for everyone—plaintiffs and defendants alike. Plaintiffs want quick settlements today and defendants want insulation from bankrupting awards for pain and suffering and punitive damages. If we had one unified, coordinated system, both of these goals could be achieved and all that would be lost would be legal "friction,"—something akin to the loss of power between the boiler and drive shaft of a steam engine.

Every court system chooses every day between the fireside equities and Pandora's box, but the calculations differ dramatically when both the fireside equities and Pandora's box are within one state, as opposed to situations where the fireside equities are at home but Pandora's box will be opened in another state half a continent away. A good example of a situation where both the fireside equities and Pandora's box are at home involves claims for workers' compensation. Workers' compensation payments are often made by national companies as the result of local, state court litigation. Workers' compensation payments, however, are based on business activities that involve the employment of local workers in the state where the workers' compensation claims are ajudicated. Every state is now desperately seeking new jobs at home; if workers' compensation costs become too high, industry will leave. Although Exxon may be a worldwide company, as far as New Jersey is concerned Exxon is a local business and a valuable community asset because of its New Jersey refineries.

There is much room for political philosophy in adjudicating workers' compensation claims because the contested cases involve wildly divergent, highly subjective, expert opinion testimony. Lawyers for plaintiffs have stables of doctors who will testify that, because a worker's thumb was crushed by a hammer, the worker now suffers a total permanent disability stemming from related psychological complications. Employers, on the other hand, have doctors who will examine a person with an eighth-grade education who has lost one arm and one foot, and who will then testify that the person is perfectly employable. When times are hard and jobs are scarce, there is an irresistible temptation to many claimants to attempt to turn any injury into a claim for a total permanent disability that will provide a pension for life. Employers respond by fighting workers' compensation cases tenaciously because the cost of workers' compensation is paid by employers through insurance premiums assessed according to each employer's individual experience. The cost of workers' compensation in the heavy chemical industry, for example, is about 6 percent of the wage bill, while in underground coal mining it may be as high as 35 percent. Consequently, whether courts are liberal or conservative in workers' compensation cases has a significant effect on total labor costs in some industries.[5]

In workers' compensation, administrative agencies as well as reviewing courts tend to be sympathetic to claimants, but their sympathy is tempered by a recognition that if awards get too generous, employers will flee across the border to states where workers' compensation payments are lower. With the Pandora's box problem in mind, I have my own idiosyncratic approach to handling the fireside equities in workers' compensation cases when the evidence allows conclusions either way. When there is a claim for psychological injury, I tend to resolve all doubt in favor of the employer. I am also reluctant to give total-disability, life awards to older workers in questionable cases because they will soon be eligible for social security and private pensions. On the other hand, with younger workers who have been seriously injured, or the widows of those who have been killed, I tend to resolve doubt in favor of the claimant. I would like to resolve every doubt in favor of the claimant, but if workers' compensation premiums get significantly out of line with similar costs in other states, heavy industry, for whom workers' compensation is a significant labor cost, will be discouraged from locating in West Virignia. It is heavy industry, after all, that provides the high-wage, unionized jobs that have tra-

5. One problem that sociologists who have studied the subject have pointed out is that in the United States disability insurance—both workers' compensation and social security—is increasingly being used as a substitute for long-term unemployment compensation. It is estimated that a significant percentage of American unemployment is disguised simply by declaring long-term unemployed workers disabled and paying them not to work, either through workers' compensation or social security. See Stone, *The Disabled State,* in chapter 2, p. 47, n. 8.

ditionally created any state's middle class, and it is heavy industry in most of urban America that also provides the lion's share of the tax base to support social services.

Thus, in the adjudication of workers' compensation claims there are strong, self-interested incentives for judges to act responsibly toward business. But the calculations in the adjudication equation change dramatically when the fireside equities occur at home whilst Pandora's box gets opened somewhere else. This is almost always the pattern in product liability cases, and it is frequently the pattern in medical malpractice and other routine tort suits. In a product liability case, the product that caused the injury is seldom manufactured in the state where the suit is brought, and most of the time the manufacturer has no business operations other than a distribution network in the state where it is being sued. In run-of-the-mill suits, such as claims arising from alleged medical malpractice or from simple automobile accidents, the plaintiff is a local resident and the *nominal* defendant is also a local resident, but the *real* defendant is a national insurance carrier.

In suits between individuals and business, or between small business and big business, the stronger party is almost always forced to rely, in one way or another, upon legislative facts rather than on fireside equities. For example, in 1986 we had a medical malpractice case in our court between the parents of a deceased child and a local doctor. The facts of the case were egregious; the doctor perforated the child's bowel while doing a routine diagnostic procedure, and then, in the face of overwhelming evidence that the child was deathly ill, failed to recognize the problem until it was too late. The child was the couple's only offspring, and the mother was unable to have any more children. Furthermore, the doctor made no reasonable settlement offer before trial, in spite of the fact that he did not even contest the issue of negligence before the jury. The jury awarded $10 million to the parents for the death of the child, but our Supreme Court of Appeals, by a 3 to 2 vote, reduced the judgment to $3 million.

At the simplest level, the defendant doctor's insurance carrier argued that $10 million was too much money, but as I listened to this argument I kept thinking of my then five-year-old son, John, and it seemed to me that if $10 million is the going rate for only children, it is too low. Two of my colleagues would have sustained the judgment entirely, but three of us reduced it by $7 million based on our understanding of legislative facts that were not even briefed by the parties, although we had explicitly invited them to do so. Our reasoning went as follows: No amount of money can compensate a parent for the loss of a child; if $10 million is not too much, then why not $100 million? We concluded that damage awards in malpractice cases are paid for by patients through the cost of medical treatment, and that, beyond a certain point, sustaining jury awards for enormous sums does nothing but add a Las Vegas parameter to every hospital visit.

But we allowed $3 million of the judgment to stand because we wanted to encourage out-of-court settlements. Without some terrifying consequence attendant upon a defendant's going to trial, defendants will always rely upon the delay, cost, and inconvenience of any lawsuit to wear down deserving plaintiffs into settling for pittances. The defendant's insurance carrier in the malpractice case admitted before the appellate court that $300,000 would have been a reasonable settlement, but no such offer was ever made—even on the day of trial.[6] In determining to sustain $3 million of the judgment we took the history of the settlement discussions heavily into account, which is simply another way of saying that we were looking at the total economic system, one part of which is the effect of in-court rules on out-of-court settlements. Furthermore, we explained all of this in the opinion.[7]

In the malpractice case the fireside equities were definitely against the doctor, while the conduct of the insurer generated unfathomable bad will on the part of both the local jury and the members of our court. Yet the doctor and his insurance carrier saved $7 million exclusively because of legislative facts that related directly to Pandora's box. The state supreme court understood that allowing such a large judgment to stand would distort settlement negotiations and significantly raise the cost of medical care in the long run. Although exact figures concerning the correlation between premium costs and claims paid appear to be a closely guarded secret by the insurance industry, it hardly take a Ph.D. in

---

6. In the trial of any lawsuit there are two existential moments for settlement. The first is the day the lawsuit is filed, and the second is the day before the jury is to be put in the box. Anywhere in between runs afoul of the tendency of defendants' lawyers to build files to justify large fees based on lawyer work product billed on an hourly basis. Consequently, much of the task of the law is to push parties towards settling at the first existential moment rather than the second. That allows faster compensation, reduces overall costs, and helps decongest the courts.

7. See *Roberts v. Stevens Hospital Clinic, Inc.,* 345 S.E.2d 791 W. Va. (1986).

economics to understand that the cost of malpractice awards must ultimately be passed along to someone.

The relationship of the fireside equities to Pandora's box in medical malpractice, however, is somewhat more tenuous than it is in workers' compensation. The problem is exacerbated by the lack of candor on the part of insurance companies, prompting, as it does, widespread suspicion that insurance companies are getting rich by not paying claims. In workers' compensation cases, both the employer and the employee are state residents (at least in the sense that the employer is directly contributing to the state's economy), and the correlation between claims and costs is a matter of public record. Furthermore, in workers' compensation the Pandora's box argument can be made to the legislature as well as to the courts, and it is often accepted there because one item high on legislative agenda is expanding employment opportunities.

In medical malpractice cases, however, premium costs differ among regions, based on extrapolations from experience; there is no clear equation relating past claims to future claims. Unfortunately, it is exactly this problem of statistical imprecision that allows insurance companies to accumulate the large surpluses that are so often pointed to by Ralph Nader in his capacity as advocate for outraged consumers. More to the point, however, a state court can't infer that conservative, judge-made malpractice law will automatically translate into lower costs for the consumers located in the state where the court sits. Experience instructs us that there are a number of possible slips between conservative tort law and the consumer's pocket. The insurance carriers can continue to base their premiums on national, rather than on local experience, which means that local health providers will pay the same premiums under conservative tort law as their colleagues across the state line pay under liberal tort law. If this occurs, the insurance companies simply make more money at the expense of injured victims—politically the least attractive of all possible outcomes. But another, and almost equally poor outcome, is that local health providers will actually pay lower premiums but will not pass them along to the consumer because there is no real price competition in many parts of the health care industry.

Yet, in the $10 million malpractice case, our court was more impressed with local policy considerations than we would have been had the same judgment been rendered in a product liability case. From what I know about myself and my colleagues, I have the distinct impression that in a product liability case the vote would have been 3 to 2 the other way, and the whole $10 million judgment would have been sustained. Had a defective Ford automobile killed the little boy, even I would have had none of the enthusiasm for reducing the judgment that I had when the judgment against the defendants would affect business and consumer costs in West Virginia. What do I care about the Ford Motor Company? To my knowledge Ford employs no one in West Virginia in its manufacturing processes, and except for selling cars in West Virginia, it is not a West Virginia taxpayer. Thus my concern for the Ford Motor Company rises to about as high a level as a Michigan supreme court justice's concern for a West Virginia glass manufacturer whose bottle explodes, injuring a Michigan resident. Neither the West Virginia court nor the Michigan court gives a healthy damn if Pandora's box is going to be opened in the other state.

But if it appears that local state courts are indifferent to the plight of out-of-state manufacturers, judges are paradigms of concern when compared to local state legislators. Even in the highly industrialized, manufacturing states like Michigan or (surprisingly) South Carolina, less than 5 percent of the product liability suits are brought against *local* manufacturers. As far as any elected legislator is concerned, then, generating more conservative product liability rules is the no-win political exercise of redistributing wealth from local residents to out-of-state business. On those rare occasions when the defendant business is local, juries often take Pandora's box factors into account and go easy on local employers. We recently had such a case in federal court in West Virginia between Monsanto, a local employer, and workers who had allegedly been injured by chemicals in the workplace. The jury found for Monsanto after a trial lasting almost six months.

Although as a judge I may be indifferent to the plight of Michigan's Ford Motor Company, I am not at all indifferent to the plight of West Virginia companies when they get hauled into court in other states. Consequently, in a broad way I am concerned about the total problem, but from a practical point of view that is like being concerned that the world once again faces an ice age. The fact of the matter is that as a state judge I can do nothing to make the overall law more sensitive to concerns of national economic policy. The best that I can do, and I do it all the time, is make sure that my own state's residents get more money out of Michigan than Michigan residents get out of us. This I call the competitive race to the bottom and it is at the heart of the structural problems presented by uncoordinated local jurisdictions.

The situation would not even be helped if a group of responsible state judges met at the National Center for State Courts in Williamsburg to see if they could call a halt to the competitive race to the bottom. The reason is that under American law a manufacturer of a product can be sued anywhere that the manufacturer can be found, and a manufacturer can be found anywhere that it "does business." The definition of "doing business" is pretty broad; almost any commercial activity other than simply sending orders into a state can be construed as "doing business" in that state. Thus, if a company has just one traveling salesman selling part-time in a state, it "does business" there for the purpose of being sued.

Fantasizing for a moment about an utterly impossible situation, we might ask hypothetically what would happen if a majority of state supreme court justices met and determined that all the state courts represented at the meeting would simultaneously narrow product liability law? The answer is that nothing would happen, because if just one or two states refused to join the compact, most of the product liability suits would be brought in those states, providing them with a new industry—court cases. We can even remember the days when Nevada was in the court case business with its easy divorce laws. Nevada residents, from lawyers to hotel keepers, made a lot of money in the divorce business.[8]

Of course state courts don't enter into interstate compacts, or even into informal agreements with the courts of other states. But it tells us something about how serious a problem the competitive race to the bottom is when we recognize that a majority of state judges could not develop a system for acting responsibly even if

8. The knowledgeable reader might suggest that under traditional conflict-of-laws rules a foreign jurisdiction in which a manufacturer is sued would be obliged to apply the law of the state where the injury occurred. That is, indeed, one ancient pillar of conflict-of-laws doctrine, but it is not the only pillar and there are lots of ways around it. Nothing in the U.S. Constitution requires a forum state to give the *laws* of the other states full faith and credit, and when a state thinks that the law of a foreign state is too conservative or too liberal for it, it simply declares the enforcement of that law contrary to its own public policy. Perfectly legal gambling debts contracted in Nevada, for example, cannot be collected in the courts of most other American states, which is why breaking both the debtor's legs is so frequently preferred to litigation by gambling *cognoscenti*.

they were determined to do so, and even if they could arrive at some consensus concerning the proper approach to the problem.

Product liability law is, perhaps, the purest example of how lack of coordination among separate, independent state courts leads ineluctably to legal results that are unfavorable to business, but it is far from being the only example. The simplest solution to this very thorny problem is direct intervention by the federal courts. Furthermore, we know from experience that such a solution will work, because in one potential competitive race to the bottom—namely, the taxation of interstate business—the federal courts have acted expertly, decisively, and provided almost a 100 percent perfect result.

Taxation of interstate business has always been a mind-boggling problem in the United States. If each state were left to its own devices, simple political dynamics dictate that each state would tax goods made in other states more heavily than goods made locally. This would give local manufacturers a competitive advantage, and it would exact revenue from entities that could not respond politically. Similarly, states that have a natural advantage in the production of some desirable commodity—as West Virginia does with electricity because of its local coal reserves—would exploit inelasticities of demand by taxing out-of-state sales of that commodity more heavily than in-state sales. Fortunately, the federal courts have met with considerable success in checking the potentially chaotic and disastrous effects of these natural dynamics. The U.S. Supreme Court's success in this endeavor can be attributed to the vision of a rational, national economy embodied in the commerce and due process clauses of the U.S. Constitution.

Of the approximately 150 cases that the U.S. Supreme Court decides by full opinion annually, about three are directly related to the validity of state taxes as applied to interstate commerce. The fact that 2 percent of the Supreme Court's annual docket is devoted to this issue is eloquent testimony that interstate taxation questions are never settled, and that revenue-hungry states persistently devise new schemes to test the frontiers of old interstate tax law. In response the Supreme Court has developed a four-pronged test that state taxes on interstate transactions must pass in order to be valid. Under this test, the state tax: (1) must be applied to an activity with a substantial relationship to the taxing state; (2) must be fairly apportioned among the states taxing the activity; (3) must not discriminate against interstate commerce; and (4) must be fairly related to the services provided by the state. If a taxpayer can prove that a state tax violates any one of these general requirements, he can then successfully challenge the tax in court. Through application of this test, the Supreme Court has virtually eliminated all *deliberately* discriminatory taxes and compelled the states to adopt formulae for the apportionment of income and *ad valorem* taxes among the different states that seek to tax a business entity operating in interstate commerce.

Yet, despite the Herculean efforts made to avoid tax discrimination against interstate commerce, it is still often the case that an interstate business pays higher taxes than it would if all of its business operations were located entirely in one state. This intractable problem can be attributed, however, to the lack of uniformity in taxation patterns among the fifty states and not to any competitive race to the bottom. Some states, like Florida, rely heavily on real and personal property taxes but do not have individual income taxes. Other states, like New York, have substantial income taxes at both the state and local levels, but do not have personal property taxes.

Business entities are taxed in a staggering variety of ways. Most states have some type of sales tax at the retail level. States also tax business income, using an income tax or a gross receipts tax. This latter tax is imposed regardless of whether the taxed business is making a profit. The theory of gross receipts taxes is that the state must provide services for state businesses and their employees regardless of whether the businesses are profitable; therefore, business must pay for government services just as it pays for raw materials or electricity.

A significant problem resulting from the lack of uniformity in state taxation arises when different states impose different types of taxes on a single activity in interstate commerce. Assume, for example, that there is a manufacturer of prefabricated steel bridges in state A that sells its product, fully erected, in state B. Assume further that state A relies for most of its revenue on a property tax and a corporate income tax, while state B relies on a gross receipts tax. In this case the company located in state A and doing business in state B pays a higher overall tax than it would if all of its operations were located in one state or the other. It must pay state B a tax measured by its gross receipts from the activity of erecting the bridge—which includes the cost of the bridge itself—and it must pay state A a tax measured by its net income from activities in state A. The harshness of this result is mollified by the fact that the tax paid to state B is a cost of doing business that can be deducted from gross income for the purposes of state A's income tax. In addition, income earned exclusively as the result of activities that go on entirely in state B are not subject to state A's income tax. Nevertheless, the income derived from the manufacture of the prefabricated bridge in state A is essentially taxed twice. Net profit is taxed under state A's income tax while state B, through its business and occupation tax, taxes the gross receipts derived from the activity of erecting the bridge.

Although schemes of taxation such as those illustrated in the prefabricated bridge example undeniably impose a greater tax burden on interstate commerce than on intrastate commerce, courts have been reluctant to invalidate them. This is due, in part, to the difficulty of developing formulae for the apportionment of taxes that tax different activities. But to concede that the courts have not solved the problem perfectly does not detract from the general proposition that courts have solved the problem substantially.

For our purposes, what is most interesting about the vigorous intrusion of the U.S. Supreme Court into the field of state taxation of interstate activities is that the Court has used the commerce and due process clauses of the Constitution to circumscribe state *legislative* activity. Taxes are always imposed by legislatures and never by courts, but the U.S. Supreme Court has been able to avoid discriminatory taxation. It has done this through the application of complex accounting formulae to a hodgepodge of legislatively enacted taxes as easily as it created court-made national standards in the decisional law of criminal procedure and libel.

The Supreme Court's rules controlling taxation of interstate commerce make it easy for state judges to apply a reasoned national policy. No one is critical of state judges for simply applying the law of the land. However, in many other areas of the law where there is no nationally imposed unity, state judges are victimized by the competitive race to the bottom by being forced to do things that they know are wrong both from the perspective of sound national and sound state policy. One example from my own experience may illustrate the point: For over twenty years states and their political subdivisions have been allowed to issue low-interest, local development bonds to finance private projects. Originally, however, the use of low-interest government bonds to assist private developers was limited to the construction of facilities that, although in many respects private, were also part of comprehensive public plans, like urban renewal projects. The typical structure of a government bond issue used to assist private business is that a public entity issues bonds to construct parking garages or housing projects secured only by the anticipated revenues of the project. The public body then leases the project to a private developer, with an option to purchase for a nominal sum once the bonds have been paid off.

Originally the courts had reserved enthusiasm for such government intrusion into traditionally free-market areas like housing and parking facilities, but reluctantly accepted the local governments' argument that the projects were basically for a "public" rather than a "private" purpose because the private market was not investing in such undertakings as the renaissance of decaying urban centers.[9] From that humble beginning, however, the public bond issue scheme spread to the construction of manufacturing plants (to provide local employment), and from there to financing hotels, shopping malls, and just about anything else that local governments chose to support. At this point we began to have private economic benefits bestowed upon individuals according to political rules of patronage rather than economic rules of efficiency.

In 1980 our court had two separate cases from the cities of Huntington and Wheeling (which directly border the state of Ohio) asking us to authorize the issuance of bonds to construct large shopping malls on the West Virginia side of the Ohio River. I thought that the whole proposition was utterly outrageous both politically and commercially, since older stores in both Huntington and Wheeling had been constructed entirely with private money and would now face government-subsidized competition. Further, the new malls would not significantly augment employment in the general area, but would only redistribute it. And, finally, these malls were not part of comprehensive urban renewal plans, and their effect was likely to be a further decline in the

---

9. The source of the courts' reluctance in these matters has been the Fifth and Fourteenth Amendments to the U.S. Constitution, and their counterparts in the various state constitutions which limit the authority of the government to take private property for public use. The argument against such bond issues is that by helping some entrepreneurs with low-interest government loans, the government takes the property of other, competing entrepreneurs who lack access to such loans.

urban centers of Huntington and Wheeling. Nonetheless, I had no choice but to vote to approve the bond issues simply because of the competitive race to the bottom.

The mall developers made convincing cases that if West Virginia did not provide them with low-interest money, they would simply cross the Ohio River and construct their malls in Ohio, where they would still draw as many West Virginia residents as they would if the malls were constructed in West Virginia. The private sector stores in West Virginia were destined to suffer the same loss of business no matter on which side of the river the malls were built, but if our court declined to allow the bonds to be issued, Ohio—and not West Virginia—would get the taxes and most of the jobs. What choice did the West Virginia supreme court have but to approve the project? We had no assurance that if our court acted responsibly the Ohio supreme court would follow suit; in fact, we rather suspected that Ohio would be pleased to take advantage of our conservatism and approve the project in Ohio. I wrote a concurring opinion pointing out that if the mall developers had proposed a similar project in the center of West Virginia, where competition from other states would not be a consideration, I would not vote to approve such a scheme.[10]

Perhaps I am wrong about the value of government-subsidized malls; maybe the short-run employment effect of constructing these behemoths is so much in the public interest that they should be approved everywhere. The point is not whether I was right or wrong in some absolute sense about the advisability of allowing such facilities to be built on a taxpayer-subsidized basis. Rather, the point is that *my best judgment* was that government should not selectively help private entrepreneurs unless there is a far more compelling social purpose than the one disclosed by the Huntington and Wheeling malls. Yet, contrary to my own best judgment, I was coerced into making what I still think is irresponsible state constitutional law simply because there was no authoritative, na-

10. For those unfamiliar with the issuance of public bonds it may seem strange that a court would be asked for approval before bonds can be issued. The reason such approval is required, however, is that public bond issues are often challenged in court, and if the court finds that a bond issue has failed to meet applicable legal criteria, the court can declare the issue void, to the ruin of the bondholders. To avoid this potential problem, bond counsel demand a court opinion on the legitimacy of any novel public bond issue before allowing the bonds to be sold.

tional standard that would foreclose greedy, adjoining states from profiting from West Virginia's integrity and thereby damaging my state's economic interests.

It should be obvious that, when I urge the development of a federal common law for business, I am not advocating a wholesale federalization of all business-related law. In fact, the need for unifying national law is comparatively limited, and whether the federal courts should undertake to assert a unifying authority in any particular area can be determined entirely by reference to current downwardly competitive patterns of behavior that inevitably arise from fifty-two separate state jurisdictions. In this regard I have attempted to present three paradigms—white, black, and gray. The white paradigm is workers' compensation where both "fireside equity" plaintiffs and "Pandora's box" defendants live, vote, and make campaign contributions in the same state. In this "white" situation, there is no reason why the proper balance between policies favoring redistribution of the wealth, and policies favoring economic growth, cannot be reconciled satisfactorily at the local level.

The black paradigm is exemplified by product liability, taxation of interstate commerce, and authorization of public bonds for private economic benefit. In the black paradigm the structure of separate, independent court systems leads inevitably to a competitive race to the bottom. In product liability, because state courts cannot tinker at national economic policy in any meaningful way, the only thing that state courts can do is assure their respective citizens of the redistribution of as much wealth in their direction from out-of-state corporations as will be redistributed the other way around. Here the most redistribution-oriented state court will inevitably set the example, which accounts for the observed phenomenon that the law is becoming progressively more redistribution-oriented and less economic-growth–oriented in any area where the black paradigm exists and the federal courts have exerted no control.

In the instance of state issuance of low-interest government bonds to construct private projects, no state court system can act responsibly in the face of irresponsibility on the part of any neighboring state. For example, although a government-subsidized factory will unfairly compete with factories constructed in the private sector, it does a New Jersey court no good at all to prohibit such a factory's being built in New Jersey if either New York or Pennsyl-

vania will take advantage of New Jersey's responsibility by shag-
ging the factory and its jobs for their states. The capacity of the
federal courts to control the downwardly competitive pressures of
the black paradigm is proven by federal court regulation of state
taxation of interstate commerce.

In the taxation of interstate commerce, local political pressures,
if left unchecked, would inevitably lead every state to impose
higher taxes on goods manufactured out-of-state than on locally
manufactured goods, and to tax out-of-state sales of locally made
products with inelastic demands at higher rates than in-state sales.
Were it not for the early intrusion of the U.S. Supreme Court into
this area, and its continuing energetic invalidation of downwardly
competitive taxing schemes, the structural dynamics of separate
jurisdictions would have led to a significant reduction in the efficiency of the American free-trade zone.

Finally, the gray paradigm involves medical malpractice and
other run-of-the-mill torts, where the plaintiffs are local residents
but the deep pocket defendants are national insurance companies. To the extent that insurers calculate their premiums on the
basis of experience in individual states, the value of federal standards *per se* in common tort law appears to be negligible. But to
the extent that companies base premiums on national or regional
experience, the same structural problems of anti-business dynamics that arise in product liability plague common tort law.

Whether any particular area of business-related law should be
federalized is not a question of political philosophy or legal principles; it is entirely a question of fact. When the sociological dynamics of separate, unrelated court systems make it *impossible* for
courts to follow a rational, national industrial policy, then the
Constitution's commerce clause implies that federal control of the
subject—either through the courts or Congress—is appropriate.
But because, as I shall now show, it is eminently unlikely that useful
legislation will come from Congress, the burden of law unification—implying as it does at least an implicit industrial policy—
must fall on the federal courts.

Chapter 4

Kiss Congress Goodbye

The competitive race to the bottom is such an obvious problem that we would expect Congress to have done something about it long ago. The fact that Congress has done nothing is eloquent testimony to our political system's bias towards the *status quo.* Irrational though the competitive race to the bottom may be, it still leads to specific political results (like the redistribution of wealth) that are of benefit to certain constituencies. For example, Congress has had product liability reform bills before it for more than ten years, yet no version has ever come close to passing both houses (although the Senate gave serious attention to the 1986 version of the bill). The reason, of course, is that the American Trial Lawyers Association and other advocates for consumers violently oppose any modification of the current, plaintiff-oriented, state systems.

Only people who believe in Tinker Bell have any firm expectation that Congress will do anything about the business problems that come out of America's fifty-three separate, competitive legal systems. Congress is simply the wrong institution on which to hang reformist hopes, because Congress is an institution deliberately, consciously, and even intelligently designed to do nothing. Stated so baldly, my summary may, perhaps, sound counter-intuitive; yet most legislation introduced in Congress is suggested by special-interest groups that are seeking to subvert the power of government, or our common treasury, to their own benefit. When it is understood that most proposed legislation is basically predatory, a do-nothing Congress seems more benign than we might at first imagine.

Because of the deliberate, inertia-prone institutional structure of Congress, a bill is unlikely to pass unless it has such overwhelming support that militant opposition can be stifled, or is so much for mother, God, and flag that it has no opposition at all. Bills that would establish uniform, national standards in product liability law and other business-related fields (under the broad authority of the Constitution's commerce clause) fall into neither category. Because law-unification bills have a significant special-interest component, they will be strenuously opposed by the adversaries of business (the trial lawyers, for example); and, because they are narrow and technical, they will never achieve sufficient political visibility to generate popular support.

Another reason that Congress will not give us relief in the area of product liability is that the problems created by separate state court systems are too complicated to be handled by any statute or group of statutes, no matter how detailed. And the two reasons for congressional inactivity—namely, the inertia-prone structure of Congress and the complexity of the subject matter—reinforce one another. Thus, if the internal structure of Congress were less Byzantine, and there were fewer obstacles on the way from a bill's introduction to a record floor vote, business might muscle through a largely favorable package of legislation. Conversely, if the issues were not as complex as they are, business and its adversaries might compromise in a number of linked areas and pass bills on law unification as parts of larger packages. But all of that is in the land of "if we had some ham, we could have some ham and eggs, if we had some eggs." In practical politics we must work with what we have, and in the case of law unification that means working with the federal courts.

Certainly the most serious problems of legal chaos for business arise in tort law generally, which includes not only product liability, but other types of liability, spanning the gamut from medical malpractice to an apartment owner's responsibility for injuries to children from seesaws and swings. Yet striking the right balance in tort law is among the most difficult tasks imaginable for anyone who does not start with a preconceived, special-interest political goal. As a judge I have always been in that unenviable position, and I am constantly perplexed. Better than the type of scholarly discussions that we regularly find in the legal literature, one humble example from my own recent experience may by itself bring home just how elusive bright-line rules are in torts.

My son John is now six years old and I constantly seek opportunities to do things with him. This quest is made a bit difficult for me because I have the athletic prowess of a turtle. Yet one of my few sportive accomplishments is a limited mastery of horsemanship. Horse riding is the ideal sport for politicians because at its heart is the skill of convincing the horse to do all the work. But unlike most people who have ridden all of their lives, I have never wanted (as an adult) to own a horse. I like to ride them; I don't like to take care of them. Owning a horse is like having your mother-in-law come to live with you permanently, and years ago I discovered that there are far more good horses in the world than there are acceptable riders. Consequently, even a mediocre rider (but not a beginner) is always welcome to exercise other peoples' horses—he is received rather like a suitor inviting someone else's widowed mother-in-law out to dinner. My own reluctance to own a horse, then, leads me to need a good livery stable that has patient, well-behaved school horses so that I can teach John to ride.

In Charleston there is a Czechoslovakian refugee who operates a boarding stable. His horses are good and their treatment is superb, which means that they tend to have surpassingly mellow dispositions, and thus are ideal horses for young, inexperienced riders. Unfortunately, my Czech friend is reluctant to rent any of his horses for riding school purposes because he cannot get insurance to cover his liability. The last quoted premium for a comprehensive liability policy was roughly $17,000 a year—more than his annual net profit from the whole business. I am outraged because I know that a person's chance of being seriously injured riding a horse is no higher than if he were playing football or skiing, yet while school districts and huge ski resorts can afford insurance, a little stable cannot. Furthermore, under existing law it is nigh impossible for a parent to agree to "assume the risk" on behalf of a minor and relieve the stable owner of liability. Small stables, therefore, are being put out of business, which means that subteen-aged children won't have healthy places to hang out where they can learn about animals.

In my own quest for good school horses, however, I have been both resourceful and undaunted. Fortunately for John and me, we spend every summer in Sarlat, France, where the large number of tourists attracted by the Dordogne river valley makes possible a flourishing livery stable industry. French liability law is distinctly undeveloped, so it is easy to find good horses for rent, cheap. All during August 1986, John and I rode for an hour each day. Indeed, he fell off his horse twice during the month and had numerous further close calls. But everyone who rides falls, whether he's six or forty-six. Horses are not like cars; they are inherently capricious and unreliable, so most of horsemanship involves keeping them from doing irrational and unauthorized things. John is now comfortable around horses, which brings me to the second part of my tale.

When we left Sarlat we went to spend a week in Paris. For John, at least, one of the obligatory incidents of any Paris visit is a trip to the Eiffel Tower. Behind the Eiffel Tower there is a large park, and after our inspection of the Paris panorama from the tower, we went for a walk in the park. There, lo and behold, were five ponies tied to a post in the middle of the public promenade for the obvious purpose of giving children pony rides. John took off immediately in the direction of the ponies, and because I have drilled into him that one never walks behind a horse, he carefully approached the cute little fellows from the side. Of course, a more miserable collection of vicious beasts could not have been imagined. Just as John approached them, they deliberately turned their tails towards him and two of them simultaneously kicked him squarely in the torso. Had they hit him in the head, they might have killed him!

To my unfathomable outrage, it was general knowledge to everyone who worked in the park that the ponies were vicious; yet, although five ponies standing in the middle of a public park must be the archetypal "attractive nuisance," the owner made no effort to protect children from them. As the nearby ice-cream seller pointed out to me, the ponies' owner was substantially dumber than the ponies. Fortunately John was not hurt, but the incident impressed upon me how difficult it is to achieve the correct balance in tort law. Had the ponies been in the United States they would have been well fenced, and any contact between children and the ponies would have been carefully supervised. More to the point, however, ponies who regularly kick would not be used in this country for anything but glue. The problem of the complete stupidity of the pony operator would be solved here by the liability of the public park for the negligence of its concessionaire—particularly if the negligent event were a recurring one.

From my horse-riding experience, then, I conclude that we are wrong to have a liability law that is so plaintiff-oriented that it makes it nearly impossible for riding schools to operate. Yet I also find that France is a needlessly dangerous society because its liability law is so underdeveloped that attractive nuisances, such as vicious ponies in public parks, can exist with impunity. It is easy to grasp intuitively the distinction between a serious accident occurring at a livery stable because a horse does something unexpected, and a serious accident occurring because vicious ponies with a history of vicious conduct kick an unsuspecting child who was attracted to them through the owner's design. But that distinction is exceedingly difficult to embody in a statute. And, to make the matter even more complicated, the same problem that existed with the ponies could occur in the setting of a livery stable (a horse, for example, with a history of running away), and a pony owner could argue that, notwithstanding the highest standard of care, he was being put out of business by the cost of liability insurance.

Historically, American courts have given up trying to make refined distinctions between ordinary livery stable horses and vicious ponies, and have said that everyone is liable if it strikes a jury to make him liable. Originally this cavalier judicial attitude toward liability was prompted by the universal availability of reasonably priced insurance. In fact, much of the theory of modern tort law, as articulated by respected academics in scholarly treatises, is that tort law's primary purpose is to insure everyone against accidental injuries. Now that liability insurance premiums are comprising a significant part of business costs, however, it becomes necessary to return to some nineteenth-century concepts (spawned at a time before insurance) of moral blame, actual negligence, assumption of risk, and unavoidable risk. Such a return, however, is structurally inhibited by the competitive race to the bottom.

Product liability law simply presents a grander version of all of the problems that my livery stable / vicious pony example presents. Although product liability is a major problem for business, few students of tort law are willing simply to curtail or eliminate product liability across the board. Even the business-sponsored product liability bills in Congress make no effort to retreat from business's responsibility for dangerous products. Rather, the focus of these bills is on the measure of damages. The reason for this moderation, of course, has to do with our commonsense notions of who should bear the burden of unavoidable risks, and of the most practical way of reducing avoidable risks. Ordinarily, for example, automobiles can be relied upon to do more or less what they are designed to do. We expect them to break down in a benign sort of way, but we do not expect wheels to come flying off as we round curves doing 65 m.p.h. Although we don't have the technology to produce an affordable car that will give us a hundred thousand miles without a repair, we do have the technology to make wheels that will stay on for half a million miles. When, therefore, a wheel falls off, causing a serious injury, even Ayn Rand's heirs as well as card-carrying members of the John Birch Society feel entitled to sue the manufacturer.

But what happens when a farmer is injured because his tractor, which has not been equipped with a roll bar, turns over, injuring him? Here we have a situation like my going to the livery stable with son John. Farmers hate roll bars, and most of them won't buy tractors that are equipped with roll bars because roll bars make getting on and off tractors more difficult. Although farmers misjudge slopes all the time and roll their tractors, most harbor an abiding conviction that they are not stupid enough to do so. It seems unreasonable, therefore, to say that manufacturers have produced an inherently dangerous product when they fail to provide roll bars on their tractors; yet some courts applying state law have held exactly that.[1]

The biggest problem in product liability law, then, is the tendency to carry a good thing too far. And, of course, this tendency is aggravated by the interstate nature of most product liability suits. The ultimate logic of product liability would imply that restaurants should be liable for heart conditions when they serve red meat instead of fish. Of course, this very logic is at the heart of suits against tobacco manufacturers for causing lung cancer with cigarettes. So far no plaintiff has won a lung cancer case, but suits

---

1. A good example of this problem is found in *Hammond v. International Harvester Co.*, 691 F.2d 646 (3rd Cir. 1982), where the widow of a farm laborer sued because a tractor lacked a roll bar. The tractor in question, an International Harvester Front End Skid Loader-Series 3300, came equipped with a roll bar, but the manager of the farm had specifically requested that the roll bar be removed by the dealer. Harvester admitted that the accident would not have occurred if the tractor had been equipped with a roll bar, and at trial the jury returned a verdict for the plaintiff. The Court of Appeals affirmed the jury's verdict and held that the tractor was unreasonably dangerous, even though it had been delivered that way *at the express direction of the purchaser.*

on the subject arise with great regularity and it seems inevitable that eventually a plaintiff will win.

Once we explore the complexity of product liability issues, it becomes obvious that the battle over tort law does not boil down to confrontations between right and wrong, but rather to confrontations between right and right. Such confrontations are distinctly unsuited to being decisively resolved in Congress—or in any other legislative body—because the partisans of change cannot command strong enough support to overcome the institutional hurdles that strongly favor the *status quo*.

I asserted that Congress is an institution deliberately, consciously, and even intelligently designed to do nothing. I have always suspected that public support for judicial activism in the United States is largely the result of an unarticulated, but nonetheless near-universal recognition of the structural limitations of all legislatures, particularly Congress. Because I advocate the development of a court-made, unifying federal common law in such areas as product liability, it is important to demonstrate here why a resort to the courts for this purpose does not confound the proper balance of power between appointed and elected branches. In this regard we should always keep in mind that our system, from its very beginning, was conceived with the tacit assumption that much law-making would be done by courts. In the English system that we inherited at the time of the American Revolution it was explicitly recognized by Parliament, at least from the passage of the Statute of Westminster II in 1285, that crafting the law governing private transactions is often done better by courts than by legislatures.[2]

There is a general rule among historians and political scientists that after any revolution the government that the revolutionaries set up will look more or less like the government before the revolu-

2. The Statute of Westminster II relaxed the Provisions of Oxford passed in 1258 that had curtailed the authority of the Lord Chancellor to issue new writs to bring new types of disputes before the royal courts. Until 1258 litigants could apply to the Lord Chancellor for a writ authorizing a royal court to decide a particular dispute, and the decision to grant a new writ was what we would call today the creation of a new cause of action. The efforts of the Provisions of Oxford to limit the lawmaking flexibility of courts proved impractical, so the Statute of Westminster II authorized the chancellor to issue new writs in *consimilis casus* (similar situations). It was under this authority, for example, that writs for "trespass" were converted into writs for "trespass on the case" (in other words, trespass in a similar case) and the modern law of negligence was born.

tion.[3] Certainly that was the way things happened after the American Revolution—the separate states continued to have governments designed along English lines. A major part of the English system was the power of courts to make law regarding all private rights not regulated by Parliament. For example, at the very time that the United States was taking shape as an independent country, Lord Mansfield, who died in 1793, was remaking the commercial law of England. American judges borrowed heavily from Lord Mansfield's decisions, in spite of the fact that they came *after* English common law was technically "received" by the separate states. Consequently, it is logical to infer that when Article 3 of the U.S. *Constitution* was drafted it was assumed by the Founding Fathers that the federal courts established by that article would have *some* lawmaking power; however, there was certainly no consensus concerning the extent of that power. But the lawyers among the founders probably understood that the lawmaking power of courts provided a necessary counterweight to the inertia of legislatures.

The institution of Congress has the same type of historical ties to English institutions that the courts have. America's expectations about what Congress would do and how it would behave were conditioned by centuries of experience with the English Parliament. Furthermore, it was generally thought that America's Congress and the federal courts would more or less interact with one another in about the same way that England's courts and Parliament interacted. Congress, it should be remembered, in no way traces its roots to any classical ideal of participatory democracy. The fact that Congress is housed in buildings of neoclassical design conveys a false historical impression about the origin and purpose of the legislative branch in our system. Congress is a near-perfect reincarnation of a *feudal* parliament in which the Senate performs the functions of the House of Lords, and the House of Representatives performs the functions of the House of Commons.

In the early thirteenth century, when parliaments were first developing, their members were more forthright than their successors are today in announcing for all the world to hear that parlia-

3. I am indebted for this insight to my colleague, Professor Evelyn Harris of the University of Charleston, who has done extensive work—as yet unpublished—to prove this interesting thesis.

ment—now Congress—is designed to do nothing. The war cry of the priests and barons who fought for parliamentary rights in the reigns of John and Henry III was *"nolumus leges anglicae mutare!"*—traditionally translated as "the laws of England shall never change." And when medieval landowning conservatives said "never," they meant *"never!"* The original objective of a parliament, then, was not to provide leadership in the affairs of state, but rather to ensure that the executive branch did not raise taxes, needlessly go to war, disturb the traditional property rights of subjects, or give away the commonweal to friends and retainers of the king. Congress serves many of the same functions today, as a quick glance at any morning's issue of the *New York Times* will easily disclose.

The problems of a medieval member of Parliament were comparatively simple, of course, when compared to those of today's legislator. Today the forces that lead to congressional inertia are slightly different from the forces that led to the same result in the Middle Ages, but the bottom-line need for powerful and imaginative courts remains unchanged. Prominent among the things that a medieval parliamentarian did not have to put up with were single-issue constituencies, bankruptingly expensive media campaigns, and low voter turnouts that shift the balance of power toward special-interest constituencies. For example, in a typical nonpresidential year during the decade from 1978 to 1988, roughly 22 percent of the vote has turned out for primary elections; and because most places have one dominant party, office is more often won in primaries than in general elections.

When primaries determine a politician's success or failure, public office is either won or lost based on the preferences of slightly better than a mere 11 percent of the vote of just members of the majority party who are registered to vote. And a sizable proportion of that 11 percent of majority party voters is always composed of militants whose political program is simply to subvert the commonweal to their own private benefit. It requires a triumph in political engineering, as well as a healthy cynicism about the day-to-day workings of democracy, to ensure that the average citizen—who often doesn't even bother to register to vote—is protected from well-organized predators. The solution to this problem devised by Congress and the state legislatures is to create internal institutional arrangements that almost guarantee the defeat of any bill not supported by a broad consensus.

The point is perhaps proved by a quick look at some of the

militant constituencies who exert a prominent presence at the federal trough. Yuppies, for example, want lower taxes on earned income; teachers want higher pay; federal employees want bigger pensions; minorities want jobs and contracts reserved on the basis of race; employers and unions faced with foreign competition want tariffs and quotas; and defense contractors want larger military budgets. These folks do not present programs that have been incisively tailored to advance anyone's notion of "the general good." Responsible legislators are reluctant to give special interests everything that they want, but in today's Congress political responsibility and legislator job security are not necessarily compatible goals. However, to the greater glory of the political art form, the institutional structure of Congress is deliberately designed to enhance as much as possible both political responsibility and congressional job security—thus, the system designed to do nothing.

A brief description of the inertia machinery of Congress begins with that body's bicameral structure. One of the things that bicameralism does is assure us that a small clique of legislators will not gain control of the whole congressional shooting match and run their own agenda for several years. After all, each congressional chamber is managed by a leadership team composed of the presiding officer, majority leader, and committee chairmen, all of whom achieve their positions through a caucus of the majority party. Consequently, a bare majority of the majority party can dominate the legislative machinery in either house and set that house's agenda.

The leadership of the House or Senate has control over the members' budgets, committee assignments, capacity to get favorable legislation passed for constituents, and even junketing opportunities. The rule in Congress has always been that to get along one must go along.[4] Because the leadership and agenda of the Sen-

---

4. In the early 1950's, when my grandfather, M. M. Neely, was in his late seventies and a very senior U.S. Senator in terms of total number of years served, but not in terms of formal seniority because of a break in service, he took on the Senate leadership. At one point he made a speech on the Senate floor, widely reported in the press, admonishing the Senate's "insufferable windbags" to deliver their time-consuming speeches elsewhere. He told my father later that his action in attempting to reform the Senate's internal procedures was among the greatest mistakes of his political career. After his speech he lost all of his internal patronage, and couldn't even get one of his constituents hired as a Capitol elevator operator.

ate are entirely different from that of the House, a structure with two chambers guarantees that the internal, self-interested trades that are made in one chamber will not translate into legislation. Thus we see that in recent years the U.S. Senate, whose members must routinely raise large sums of money from business, has given far more serious consideration to bills limiting product liability exposure than the House, where the influence of local trial lawyers and consumer groups outweighs the money power of business. Congressmen simply can't use the same type of multimillion-dollar media blitz that works so well in statewide Senate races.

Bicameralism alone, of course, does not provide all of the inertia machinery that Congress needs to function responsibly. Therefore, within each House of Congress there is a committee system that diffuses responsibility and allows most members to appear favorably disposed towards special-interest legislation without a serious threat that such legislation will ever reach the floor where a member must make a recorded vote.

Judicial activism has probably come to be accepted as a useful part of the American political process simply because Congress is expected to perform two incompatible functions. First, Congress is expected to kill[5] predatory, special-interest legislation that does nothing more than enrich one group at the expense of another. At the same time, however, Congress is expected to pass general interest legislation designed to make the United States a more prosperous country or a more just society. Although, for the most part, general-interest legislation may have a special-interest component, and special-interest legislation may have a general-interest component, it is still possible to draw both a practical and a theoretical distinction between the two.

Unfortunately, history indicates that it is nearly impossible for a legislature to achieve a perfect balance between killing bad legislation and passing good legislation. After World War II, Norway adopted a new constitution with a unicameral legislature; but after several years of experience, the single-house Norwegian parliament divided itself voluntarily into two houses in order to achieve

5. In the world of legislators there is a significant difference between "killing" a bill and "defeating" a bill. "Killing" a bill involves the bill's silent death in the Byzantine committee process, which includes such things as lack of agreement in conference committees once different versions of the same bill have been passed by both Houses. "Defeating" a bill, on the other hand, involves voting a bill down by record vote on the floor of one House.

a better balance between passing and killing legislation. In England during the Civil War (c. 1648), when there was but one House of Parliament, the House of Commons went so wild in passing special-interest legislation that it paved the way for Cromwell's dictatorship. And when Franklin Roosevelt took office in 1933 the *zeitgeist* so encouraged Congress to be a rubber stamp for the president's programs that much bad legislation was passed. Although today we complain about "do-nothing" congresses, perhaps an overly active Congress is even more of a plague. One way, however, by which a correct balance is achieved between too much law and too little is to consign certain types of necessary lawmaking to the courts, where special-interest problems are less prominent.

Although the federal courts are not elected, and for that reason are subject to charges of arrogance and elitism, they nonetheless have few, if any, special-interest pressures on them as lawmakers.[6] The sorting out and compromising of special interests, much of which involves allocating the federal budget, is done entirely by Congress. Furthermore, for those who defend the right of Congress to make or decline to make all law, it is important to point out that Congress itself aids and abets the power of courts to craft the "general-interest" law of America. For example, Congress routinely passes *intentionally* vague legislation in the rightful expectation that the courts will give such legislation precise dimensions in the context of specific cases. This congressional *modus operandi* is particularly prominent whenever there is a clear consensus that something must be done in a given area—such as emission standards for automobiles or discrimination in private hiring—but there is no consensus concerning exactly what to do. In some instances, like environmental regulation, an administrative agency is interposed between Congress and the courts; but in other areas, like employment discrimination under Title VII of the Civil Rights Act, the courts receive the issue directly.

---

6. They do, however, have another and perhaps just as serious a problem—namely, a lack of information. The judiciary is an extremely isolated institution, and the problems of isolation become increasingly prominent as one moves up the court hierarchy to the policymaking appellate courts. Legislators are *involuntary* consumers of information because they must listen patiently to constituents, from formal appointments in their own offices to buttonholing at AFL-CIO picnics. Judges, on the other hand, are entirely *voluntary* consumers of information, because no one but close social friends, family, and staff talk to them outside the confines of formal judicial proceedings. I shall elaborate on this problem in chapter 6.

Eliminating the competitive race to the bottom that results from the conflicting state law of independent jurisdictions is theoretically a general-interest undertaking. In practice, however, law unification that changes the current system involves some realignment in the distribution of wealth that will necessarily confound numerous special interests. For example, plaintiffs' lawyers are currently quite happy with the soft rules among the separate states regarding conflict of laws—particularly because they can shop for favorable forums—and it is unlikely that any new national, uniform rule on conflicts of law would be as favorable to plaintiffs as the existing local rules.[7] If, therefore, a bill on uniform conflict-of-laws rules came up for consideration, everyone who profited from the current system would mobilize the inertia machinery in Congress to block any change.

Business, assuredly, would profit from clear, universally applied conflict-of-laws rules; but business has long agenda in other, more pressing, areas and can hardly expend its limited political capital on anything so technical as rules governing conflict of laws. No business at any one time has enough at stake in getting uniform conflict-of-laws rules to warrant the necessary lobbying effort. And, with the prominent exception of product liability law, which affects all manufacturers and distributors all of the time, the same political dynamics apply to every other discrete area of law uniformity. No one business, for example, can afford to devote money and political capital to efforts to reform the law governing the

---

7. "Conflicts of laws," to reiterate a definition given earlier in chapter 2, is simply that body of legal doctrine that determines which of two possible laws applies to a given case. For example, when the disaster at the Union Carbide plant in Bhopal, India, occurred in 1985, energetic plaintiffs' lawyers in the United States solicited clients among the injured in India with a view to bringing suit against Union Carbide in the United States. The most important questions in those suits was whether the law of India or the law of the United States would apply, and whether the actions themselves could be prosecuted in American federal courts. The United States District Court decided that, because the controlling law was Indian law, and because all the witnesses, victims, and Union Carbide management on the site were Indians, the case should proceed in the Indian courts. A further wrinkle resulted from the fact that India passed a statute after the accident giving the Indian government the exclusive right to represent all the injured victims as well as itself. However, the District Court ordered that while the cases should all be transferred to India, Union Carbide, the defendant, would be subject to certain burdensome procedural rules of U.S. courts concerning discovery, although the Indian government would not. See *In re Union Carbide,* 634 F. Supp. 842 (1986).

issuance of public bonds to support private enterprise. What chance would the merchants of Huntington and Wheeling, West Virginia, have to get such a law passed at the national level? By the time they organized their forces and found similarly situated allies, the whole question would be moot.

I will say again that the inertia-prone structure of Congress is maintained by the complexity of the task of designing a proper system of unified laws. This complexity, however, does not arise simply because it is difficult to imagine fair rules of universal application in such areas as product liability. Rather, the most intractable source of complexity lies in the fact that everything in the judicial system is interrelated, from the money appropriated to buy a judge's secretary a word processor to the exact wording of the rules of civil procedure. Overcrowded dockets can have just as dramatic an impact on the overall political result that courts give as the rules governing liability. Therefore, the entire legal system must be viewed as a whole, and, within that whole, uniformity *per se* is but one small part. But this small part may be like a tiny wheel in a mechanical watch, tinkering at which can impair the accuracy of the whole mechanism.

Somewhere in most lawyers' offices is a representation of Blind Justice standing with her eyes covered and an empty balance scale in her right hand. We would all have a better feel for the total legal system, however, if Blind Justice held a balance scale with a twenty-pound weight on each pan. The scale would still be in balance, but it wouldn't be in balance in quite the uncomplicated way that most people currently like to imagine. Certainly, it is absurd that a manufacturer can be held liable for "punitive" damages simply because there was a design defect in a product. But it is also absurd that an injured plaintiff cannot get to trial and through the appellate process in less than six years. Both punitive damages and trial delay are absurd when looked at alone, but when combined they achieve something approaching a workable balance in that most important, but perhaps least discussed, area of court endeavor—voluntary settlement. Widespread reluctance among legislators to tinker at court-related problems, therefore, is often prompted by nothing more than the fear that they might disturb a delicate balance of apparently ridiculous, but nonetheless countervailing, rules.

The balance of terror achieved by offsetting stupidities is nothing to be taken lightly. Courts, after all, are important not for the cases that they decide, but rather for the cases that they *do not* decide. Court statistics from across the country demonstrate that roughly 96 percent of all cases *filed* in court are settled before trial, and some incalculably greater number are settled after lawyers have been contacted but before formal pleadings are filed. Courts, therefore, perform a function somewhat akin to the American nuclear arsenal—through a legal phenomenon similar to mutual assured destruction, they encourage negotiation, compromise, and settlement. But all of the rules that govern in-court proceedings, as well as such extra-judicial considerations as court calendar backlog, legal fees, and the aggravation associated with litigation, combine to cast a shadow within which the great bulk of society's disputes are voluntarily settled by the parties. It is basically this shadow of the law that is the supreme political result that courts give to America.

Civil courts are in the business of redistributing wealth; when the machinery breaks down, no wealth is redistributed, which is obviously an advantage to insurance companies and other businesses that are usually defendants. Conversely, when civil courts work efficiently, plaintiffs prosper to the detriment of defendants. It should come as no surprise, then, that there are defendants' lobbies working all the time to keep courts as impotent as possible, because the way courts are organized—in terms of number of judges, delay, appeals procedure, and technical rules—has a decisive effect on the contours of the shadow of the law in which all private ordering of affairs occurs.

There is a constant war going on in American courts between plaintiffs and defendants. The war, however, is not simply a contest over the substantive rules of liability. An insurance company, for example, can achieve low settlements either when the rules of liability favor defendants, or when the courts are so backlogged that plaintiffs can't get through the system in less than six years. When the substantive rules of law go against defendants, defendants simply try to enhance the system's overall expense, complexity, and delay. At the simplest level, this involves keeping the number of available judges as small as possible, and minimizing all court logistical support.

Defendants also understand that it is always an advantage for them when court procedure is extraordinarily complicated, because complexity *per se* gives the edge to the side that has money enough to hire massive legal firepower. The tobacco companies are notorious for adopting a "whatever it takes" approach to litigating lung-cancer cases. They hire investigators to inquire into every aspect of the private lives of plaintiffs and their witnesses, and then use the discovery mechanisms available to them—such as pretrial depositions—to attempt to harass and embarrass plaintiffs into giving up. They will ask about adulterous relationships, mental illness, business problems, and personal relationships with neighbors. Almost all large defendants have stables of young, salaried lawyers who can generate mountains of obstructive and obfuscating paperwork to grind any lawsuit to a halt for years. Trial court judges simply collapse when they are inundated with hundreds of pounds of written bafflegab that they must read before deciding some technical issue. A busy trial court can take as long as a year to decide one pretrial motion if the issues are made sufficiently complicated.

On the plaintiffs' side, the intent of strategy is to make any journey into court as terrifying as possible for defendants. The plaintiffs can't beat the defendants by getting more judges because the legislatures won't appropriate the money. But the plaintiffs can get the rules on liability and damages—including the newest vogue, "punitive damages"—to be so draconian that it becomes unhealthy for defendants to linger long in court before settling. Often, defendants refuse to be terrified and go to court anyway. Sometimes defendants even win. But as the $10.53 billion judgment in the *Pennzoil v. Texaco* case demonstrates, taking too hard a line can be a bankrupting experience. Defendants learn from object lessons like *Texaco* that regardless of what they *think* the rules of law are, going to court in any case is a chancy business at best. And plaintiffs understand that the only hope that a plaintiff has for a quick settlement is to convince the defendant that if the case goes to a jury the judgment will be monstrous. Juries, after all, are famous for operating on emotive rather than legal principles, something that the *Texaco* case also amply demonstrates.

Earlier I wrote that lawyers for manufacturers are urging the federal courts to intervene in state court proceedings when there are a multiplicity of claims for punitive damages arising out of one wrongful act. Such cases usually involve the sale of a product, like the Ford Pinto, that has a design defect of which the manufacturer was aware. The standard instruction on punitive damages tells the jury that if they find intentional misconduct, or wanton and willful negligence on the manufacturer's part, they may award the plaintiff punitive damages in such an amount as to discourage the defendant and others in like circumstances from engaging in similar immoral conduct in the future. In some places, like New Jersey, the jury is instructed that they should take other lawsuits involving the same design problem into account, and award the plaintiff only his fair share of some total aggregate of punitive damages. However, even in states like New Jersey, with the law of punitive damages most favorable to manufacturers, punitive damages are still left to the discretion of the jury. The primary reason for this is that the threat of punitive damages provides a strong incentive for the defendant to settle.

Let us assume that a plaintiff has been severely injured by a product as the direct result of a design defect and that, because he is permanently disabled, his damages are legitimately half a million dollars. Why should the manufacturer pay half a million dollars promptly when it can keep its money in its pocket for up to six years? Plaintiffs who have been severely injured need money today, not six years from now. Therefore, all other things being equal, the manufacturer should be able to settle for $150,000. Furthermore, the American rule on lawyers' fees is that each side pays its own lawyers—losers don't pay for the winners' day in court.

But everybody knows that lawyers are expensive and that trying a complicated lawsuit has costs even beyond lawyers' fees. Consequently, we have devised two ways around the American rule that everyone must pay his own lawyer. The first is to allow the plaintiff to recover for subjective elements of damage like pain and suffering, and the second is to allow punitive damages in certain narrow cases. But although punitive damages are usually not recovered, the *possibility* that they *might* be recovered presents a strong incentive to prompt settlement. If, therefore, a suit that is legitimately worth $500,000 goes to trial, it is likely that a jury will award over a million dollars, part of which may well be punitive damages. Juries aren't stupid; the average juror knows from experience—either his own or his friends'—that the plaintiff must get some money to pay his lawyer about a third of the total award.

It is possible to do something about outrageous, duplicative punitive damages, but tinkering at the punitive damages rules without also tinkering at the rules governing settlement will not be politically acceptable. One example might illustrate the problem. In 1986 the West Virginia Supreme Court had an appeal by an insurance company that had been sued on a fire insurance pol-

icy by the policyholder. The policyholder recovered not only lawyers' fees for bad-faith settlement practices but punitive damages
as well.[8] The insurance company had denied coverage on a
$150,000 fire policy because it suspected arson by the owner. The
insured's building was an abandoned restaurant that had been out
of business about six months. The insurance company had discovered that the insured was in financial trouble and that the mort-
gage and other expenses of the insured building were a significant
drain on his resources. It was undisputed that the fire had been
set by an arsonist, but the owner denied that he had had anything
to do with the burning.

The policyholder sued and asked the jury not only for the face
amount of the policy, but also for lawyers' fees and punitive damages. According to the policyholder, the company failed to make
a good-faith investigation and elicited only those facts that would
support its arson charge. The jury gave the policyholder $150,000
for the building, $67,000 for lawyers' fees, and $50,000 in punitive
damages. It was a close case on the issue of arson itself, but all the
evidence against the policyholder was circumstantial. There is no
reason to believe that juries are sympathetic to arsonists, so the
jury must have been convinced by the witnesses that the policyholder was telling the truth. We substantially affirmed the case
because it was fairly tried under the old law, but we also used it
for setting a new rule on insurance claims and punitive damages.[9]

Our new rule attempted to establish bright lines that might
guide settlements. We said that in fire insurance cases, if an insurance company forces a policyholder to sue by denying a policyholder's claim, and the policyholder wins, then the company is
automatically liable for the policyholder's lawyers' fees plus damages for aggravation and inconvenience. The value of aggravation
and inconvenience is a jury question under our new rules, but
lawyers' fees are now presumptively one-third of the face amount
of the policy unless the policy is either very small or very large.
However, we now limit punitive damages to instances where the
evidence clearly, cogently, and convincingly shows that the com-

8. There are some exceptions to the general rule that losers don't pay for the
winners' lawyers. In some states one of these exceptions occurs when an insurance company engages in a bad-faith refusal to pay for a loss covered by its
policy. This result is usually based on statutory provisions that require an insurance company to settle claims in good faith.

9. *Hayseeds, Inc. v. State Farm Fire & Cas.*, 352 S.E.2d 73 (W. Va. 1986).

pany knew the claim was legitimate and deliberately denied it out of pure malice. Under the new rule such things as negligence, poor judgment, or bureaucratic incompetence on the part of the company will not give rise to a claim for punitive damages, and trial courts cannot allow juries to consider punitive damages claims unless there is clear evidence of actual malice.

The reasoning that led us to attempt a wholesale overhaul of the way property damage, fire insurance cases are tried began with the proposition that insurance contracts are now at the heart of the American commercial system. Not only insureds, but a host of third parties, like creditors, rely on them. Consequently, insurance contracts are qualitatively different from other contracts. Next we recognized that in the whole claim-submission game there are not just two players—the policyholder who wants his money, and the company that wants to do whatever will end up costing it the least money. Between these two players is a third and terribly important player—the bureaucracy of claims adjusters and insurance company lawyers whose livelihoods depend upon the litigation of claims. Such a bureaucracy is inevitable in a world fraught with false claims, and that bureaucracy is inherently neither good nor evil. But it exists, and it is subject to the same institutional dynamics for self-preservation and self-aggrandizement that plague every other bureaucracy. The trouble with insurance claims is that, without charges by the policyholder of lack of good faith, the company has little to lose and everything to gain by fighting policyholders' claims.

When a policyholder has lost everything, an intransigent insurance company can force the policyholder to settle for a pittance by threatening years of litigation and no money in the meantime. Without punitive damages or some other handle for extra compensation, even if the policyholder wins he is out his lawyers' fees and litigation costs. Our new rule recognizes that it is perfectly legitimate for an insurance company to contest a claim because of fraud, but that if it loses, the burden of litigation must be on it. Simultaneously, however, we have eliminated entirely any jeopardy whatsoever for open-ended, punitive damages unless a high threshold of intentional, malicious conduct is reached. Furthermore, we eliminated all liability hazards for the insurance company when it offers to settle a property damage claim for less than the face amount of the policy. In many jurisdictions a company's offer of settlement for less than the face amount of the policy is evidence of bad faith, but we concluded that such a rule serves no valid public policy. In cases involving circumstantial evidence, neither party may want to roll the dice in front of a jury, and so settlements should be encouraged.

Our purpose in formulating the new rules in fire insurance cases was to encourage companies to exercise greater control over their own claims settlement bureaucracies, while at the same time narrowing the hazard to companies that have legitimate reasons to deny claims. Yet it is eminently unlikely that such a bright-line rule—or any other rule—would have emerged from a legislature. The insurance companies would have fought tooth and nail against an automatic award of lawyers' fees, and the plaintiffs' lawyers would have screamed about the virtual elimination of punitive damages as an issue in a fire insurance case. In the wake of such a hot political contest over a narrow, technical matter to which the great majority of legislators are indifferent, the inertia mechanisms of the legislature would have taken over and nothing at all would have happened.

The one bill on law uniformity that has received enough serious congressional attention to have passed the Senate in 1986, namely SB 2760 on product liability, has taken a sophisticated approach to the whole settlement issue. Of the bill's forty-three printed pages, ten were devoted to an expedited settlement mechanism. Among the settlement provisions is one that allows any plaintiff who has made an offer of settlement that has been rejected by a defendant to recover lawyers' fees up to $100,000 if the plaintiff recovers in court an amount equal to or greater than his settlement offer. However, the whole settlement issue under SB 2760 is much more complicated than just arranging the payment of lawyers' fees.

Under SB 2760, a plaintiff's offer of settlement can include only damages for "net economic loss" and something called "dignitary loss," which is defined as noneconomic loss in the amount of $100,000 consisting of pain and suffering, or mental anguish, associated with (1) the death of a parent, child, or spouse; (2) serious and permanent disfigurement; (3) loss of a limb or organ; or (4) serious and permanent impairment of a bodily function. Consequently, although SB 2760 emphasized getting claims settled quickly, there was also a cap on demands for pain and suffering, as well as a narrowing of the circumstances that can give rise to a pain and suffering demand in a settlement offer. "Net economic loss," of course, consists of such things as lost wages, property damage, medical expenses, and lost earning capacity from a permanent disability.

Although SB 2760, which has been in the works in one form or another for over a decade, made a fair effort to tinker at the whole system at once in order to maintain balance, it was still a special-interest bill that severely narrowed the existing rights of plaintiffs in product liability suits. For example, an award of $100,000 for lawyers' fees is parsimonious in many product claims because just the expert witness and investigative costs may surpass that amount. Consequently, SB 2760 was not just a bill about uniformity *per se,* but rather a bill that proposed uniformity *plus* a major realignment in favor of defendants. And it is for that reason that the bill would not have passed the House in any form acceptable to manufacturers.

One reason, therefore, for consigning law uniformity issues to federal courts is that courts can manipulate more pieces of the total system at once than Congress can. Courts are more likely than Congress to achieve uniformity without the special interest effects associated with legislation. The converse of that proposition is that because a statute cannot manipulate enough parts of the product liability system simultaneously and with sufficient neutrality, a political consensus strong enough to allow a statute on product liability to pass Congress will never develop.

If the federal courts were to direct their energies towards national law unification they could achieve a revolution in ten years. If we return for a moment to the problem of a manufacturer's being sued for punitive damages simultaneously in numerous state courts, it is both a clear and fair rule to say that after the first award of punitive damages, manufacturers should be able to eliminate further punitive damages by a quick and fair settlement offer. Because punitive damages are largely designed to promote quick settlements, we should make that rationale explicit and allow manufacturers to avoid outrageous jury awards by the simple expedient of voluntarily treating victims fairly.[10] However, a

10. Perhaps the consumers' lobby can argue persuasively that some business conduct is so willful and intentional that the businesses involved should be punished into bankruptcy because they have deliberately hurt individuals. Most punitive damages cases, however, do not involve *deliberate* intent, and a narrow exception to the general rule allowing punitive damages for actual malice does no

manufacturer who wishes to relitigate his liability for a defective product, and who seeks to use the structural imperfections of the judicial system against deserving plaintiffs, should be forced to do so at his peril.

Thus, one Supreme Court opinion can establish the bright line that a manufacturer can either: (1) accept the first court decision determining that the product was defective and that the manufacturer acted recklessly, in which case the manufacturer must concede liability and be willing to settle all similar claims in good faith, but is not then liable to further punitive damages; or (2) the manufacturer may continue to litigate the whole issue of liability, in which case each new lawsuit stands or falls on its own, and, if additional punitive damages are awarded, tough luck for the manufacturer.

Such a rule provides a clear, reasonable, and uniform standard; but the reader has probably already imagined several permutations of the basic problem that the rule as simply stated does not solve. For example, suppose the accident at issue involves the explosion of the gas tank of a Ford Pinto when the car owner was trying to open his gas tank with a blowtorch. The fact that Pinto gas tanks have been determined to be defective does not mean that every accident involving one results from the design defect. If Ford wants to litigate the cause of an individual accident, does the fact that it concedes a design defect at the outset shield it from punitive damages? I would think so, but these are questions that can be solved only through case-by-case refinement of the basic, national rule.

In product liability cases it is possible to envisage numerous alternatives to the current balance-of-terror scheme, but no single state can afford to experiment because of all the problems that I described relating to the competitive race to the bottom. Yet a federal court could hold that an offer to arbitrate product claims would create a sufficient showing of good faith to insulate a manufacturer from punitive damages in cases where there is no actual

---

violence to the basic rule I propose. However, even in cases of actual malice—something that has probably been proven in the A. H. Robins Dalkon Shield case—it does plaintiffs as a class little good to put the manufacturer into bankruptcy or force it out of business. This is particularly true if the product has been widely distributed and new plaintiffs are destined to emerge years later when their injuries become apparent.

intent to cause harm.[11] In that way cases that currently clog the courts' dockets would be moved to a quicker and cheaper forum. But the forum must actually be quicker and cheaper, of course; our experience with alternatives to litigation is not particularly encouraging. For example, state workers' compensation is a nightmare everywhere, and the National Labor Relations Board is not exactly a model of quick and efficient adjudication.

Different tort liability problems demand limited, specific rules custom-crafted to solve those specific problems. As I have said, the federal courts have created narrow, specialized rules of national application for the torts of libel and slander. It is obvious that free-speech considerations make media libel and slander a unique problem, but there are countless other unique problems. For example, widespread vaccination has reduced to insignificant levels the risks of most of the dreaded childhood diseases of fifty years ago, such as diphtheria, measles, German measles, mumps, hepatitis B, influenza, and polio, to mention just a few. Recently, however, both state and federal courts have been handing down substantial judgments against the manufacturers of the Sabin polio vaccine because the vaccine induced cases of polio. The same problem is occurring with most of the other common vaccines. My own mother had polio when she was a child, and—until the Salk vaccine came on the market in the late 1950's—summer was always a frightening time for me, because each year in the United States there were more than 15,000 serious new cases of polio. The Sabin vaccine (an improvement over the earlier Salk vaccine) induces cases of polio in fewer than one in a million of those inoculated.

Today's tort liability jeopardizes universal inoculation because large judgments, large settlements, and just the litigation costs

11. It is difficult to define the point at which intention to profit from a product known to be less than ideally safe becomes actual malice. For example, it was generally recognized that it was less safe to crash in a Volkswagen Beetle than in a Volvo 145 E. However, the fact that Volkswagen knew the Beetle to be one of the least crashworthy cars on the market and continued to sell it does not imply that the sale of the Beetle was malicious. The very appearance of the Beetle put the public on notice that it was safer to crash in the 145 E. The consumer balanced the safety factor when he decided whether to buy the 145 E or the less expensive Beetle.

However, were a manufacturer to market a car that it knew would explode, killing all passengers on impact, and continue to market the car despite its knowledge of that danger and the public's lack of such knowledge, the sale of that car would be malicious.

themselves significantly raise the price of vaccines. According to the Harvard Medical School, rates of immunization are as low as 60 percent in some communities—particularly in poor communities where ignorance, overcrowding, and poor sanitation place children at high risk. People have little incentive to pay high prices for immunization when a disease has been virtually eradicated, but failure to maintain high levels of immunization almost guarantees that once-dreaded diseases will reappear. Certainly, this is a situation that approaches in urgency some of the free-speech problems that prompted special rules for libel and slander.

Encouraging the production of cheap, safe vaccines, then, is a desirable national policy and it must be implemented at the national level. Yet because there is no significant political constituency that cares about the problem, Congress is unlikely to open up the whole product liability can of worms just to extract this one individual worm, important though it is. H. R. 5186, signed by the president on 14 November 1986, addresses itself to the vaccine problem, but its approach is more cosmetic than substantive. In comparison to the way the Supreme Court handled media libel problems, the vaccine bill is like a pistol compared to the battleship *Missouri*.

One reason that courts are superior to Congress for law uniformity purposes is that courts spend all their days worrying about individual worms, and dealing with one worm does not necessarily imply that courts must deal with all the others. All of this will become obvious in a moment when we review how the Supreme Court dispatched the libel problem. The same capacity to be incisive does not exist in Congress because of the amendment process, the need for political trades, and the general rather than context-specific nature of most legislation.

In my estimation, next to establishing national rules on state taxation of interstate business, the Supreme Court's most successful foray into law unification has been the national law of libel and slander involving the media. To understand what occurred, it is necessary to return for a moment to the 1960's when political controversies among American regions created a hazard to national media companies similar to the hazards experienced by vaccine manufacturers today.

In 1960 the Committee to Defend Martin Luther King and the Struggle for Freedom in the South bought a full-page advertisement in the *New York Times* in which the committee made patently untrue allegations about the conduct of the Montgomery, Alabama, police department during civil rights protests. Among the false statements in the advertisement was one that said: "In Montgomery, Alabama, after students sang 'My Country Tis of Thee' on the State Capitol steps, their leaders were expelled from school, and truckloads of police armed with shotguns and tear gas ringed the Alabama State College Campus." L. B. Sullivan, one of three elected commissioners of the City of Montgomery, Alabama, and the supervisor of that city's police department, sued the *New York Times* and the committee for libel. The Alabama courts found the statements both false and libelous and awarded Commissioner Sullivan $500,000 in damages.

The *New York Times* appealed to the U.S. Supreme Court, and in March 1964 the Supreme Court rendered its opinion in *New York Times v. Sullivan*—the case that began Supreme Court supervision of all matters in state courts relating to freedom of speech involving media defendants. The Supreme Court held that the First Amendment to the U.S. *Constitution* precludes state court libel judgments against newspapers for publishing false statements about public officials unless a newspaper either knows at the time of publication that the statements are false or behaves with reckless disregard of the truth.

The liberal media usually characterize *Times v. Sullivan* as a case about our constitutional right to free speech, but it is also an important business case. Without touching in the least regard any other state tort law, *Times v. Sullivan* eliminated in one stroke the only "product liability" hazard that threatens the media industry. It is for this reason that I believe vaccine manufacturers will have a better chance in the Supreme Court than they will ever have in Congress. The Supreme Court preempted state libel law, and in its place imposed a uniform national standard of liability with a very high threshold. *Times v. Sullivan* hence opened up virtually unlimited profit-making opportunities for newspapers, magazines, and broadcasters. In fact, the profit opportunities for local newspapers are such that in 1987 the going rate for local papers sold to chains like Gannett was roughly $1,500 per subscriber. Furthermore, to make the profit picture better, logical extensions of the *Sullivan* doctrine have led to special procedural rules in libel cases—such as the liberal granting of summary judgments—that protect the media from the bankrupting effects of accumulating legal fees.

For our purposes here, the remarkable thing about Supreme Court control of state libel law is how infrequently the Supreme Court must reverse state court judgments. Although, immediately after *Times v. Sullivan* was decided, numerous libel and slander cases reached the Supreme Court, in the last ten years the Court has averaged fewer than two such cases a year. The reason is that the state trial courts now give the instructions required by federal constitutional law to local juries, which generally follow the law and find for the media defendants. When juries fail to follow the law, the state appellate courts overturn the trial court judgments, which means that few libel cases are incorrectly decided at the state level. Yet Supreme Court specialists agree that cases in which substantial judgments are allowed to stand against media defendants in state courts are among the cases most thoroughly scrutinized by the Supreme Court when screening applications for appeals. It is probably for this reason that state appellate courts save themselves the embarrassment of reversals by carefully following the law laid down by the Supreme Court.

The one thing that I have learned as a judge is that judges are politicians and not scholars or scientists. When judges come collectively to believe that something is a good idea—whether it be integration, the reapportionment of both houses of state legislatures on the basis of population, abortion on demand, or protection of the media from libel—that something quickly becomes law. I now want to turn to the ample precedent in the American federal system for a national common law on product liability matters. It is simply a question of persuading judges that such a common law is a good idea.

Chapter 5

Mother, God, and Federalism

Federalism, of course, is one of those things—like Mother and God—that we are all *required* to love. Some of the most arcane but heated discussions at political science conferences concern the role of federalism in modern American government. Yet even those who, deep in their hearts, find federalism a bothersome anachronism still pay lip service to the principle. The legal literature is full of articles with titles like "The Death of Federalism," "The Second Death of Federalism," and "The Third Death of Federalism."

Whenever I become embroiled in academic discussions about federalism, it comforts me to remember a particularly elegant passage from Macaulay's *The History of England:*

> The science of politics bears in one respect a close analogy to the science of Mechanics. The mathematician can easily demonstrate that a certain power, applied by means of a certain lever or a certain system of pulleys, will suffice to raise a certain weight. But his demonstration proceeds on the supposition that the machinery is such as no load will bend or break. If the engineer, who has to lift a great mass of real granite by the instrumentality of real timber and real hemp, should absolutely rely on the propositions which he finds in treatises on Dynamics, and should make no allowance for the imperfections of his materials, his whole apparatus of beams, wheels, and ropes would soon come down in ruin, and with all his skill, he would be found a far inferior builder to those painted barbarians who, though they never heard of the parallelogram of forces, managed to pile up Stonehenge. What the engineer is

to the mathematician, the active statesman is to the
contemplative statesman. It is indeed most important that
legislators and administrators should be versed in the
philosophy of government, as it is most important that the
architect, who has to fix an obelisk on its pedestal, or to hang a
tubular bridge over an estuary, should be versed in the
philosophy of equilibrium and motion. But, as he who has
actually to build must bear in mind many things never noticed
by d'Alembert and Euler, so must he who has actually to govern
be perpetually guided by considerations to which no allusion
can be found in the writings of Adam Smith or Jeremy
Bentham. The perfect lawgiver is a just temper between the
mere man of theory, who can see nothing but general
principles, and the mere man of business, who can see nothing
but particular circumstances.

Obviously the single most compelling argument against a federal common law springs from concepts of state sovereignty. Consequently, it becomes necessary to meet federalism objections to a
national common law in interstate matters. But here, I must con-
fess, I repair to the wisdom of Macaulay who talks about lifting a
great mass of real granite. If, to use Macaulay's metaphor, those
who wish to raise the federalism objection insist on relying entirely on the propositions that they find in treatises on political
dynamics, and insist on the supposition that the machinery is such
that no load will bend or break it, then everything that follows will
be unconvincing.

I make no claim to having reconciled state sovereignty with a
national law. Fortunately, I am an elected state judge advocating
greater national uniformity in law, and that consideration, I hope,
lends my advocacy a certain credibility. I suspect that I would be
taken less seriously if I were a federal judge. Objections to a national law based on federalism are refuted to my satisfaction if it
can be shown that the benefits we currently derive from federalism will not be jeopardized by national law while new, valuable
benefits will follow. Theoretical consistency for its own sake in all
federal-state relations is more trouble than it is worth—and this is
not cynicism, but traditional American pragmatism.

In my experience, arguments for federalism can be divided into
three broad categories: (1) historical federalism; (2) result-oriented
federalism; and (3) practical federalism. Of the three, the easiest
to dispatch for our purposes here is historical federalism. There

is little doubt that the men who drafted and ratified the *Constitution of the United States* did not envisage a strong, centralized, national government. The *Constitution's* framers and other professional politicians of the time might, indeed, have perceived the national government as potentially a stronger institution than the ordinary voter perceived it to be, but the need to amend the original document with a specific Bill of Rights to secure ratification shows how unenthusiastic the common people were about centralized power. All of that, however, was 200 years ago, and historical federalism has been repealed by history. Much of that repeal occurred at the time of the Civil War when the Thirteenth and Fourteenth Amendments to the *Constitution* were passed, conferring broad, new powers on the federal government. But the legal arguments based on minor changes in the constitutional document have less to do with historical federalism's repeal than a basic change in the way people perceive the federal government. Today public opinion polls show that the average voter thinks more highly of the honesty, capacity, and efficiency of the federal government than he does of either state or local government.

When today's political science professors point out that the federal government is a government of "delegated" powers, we all chuckle because by common consent state power has become more a matter of administrative convenience than an element of sovereignty. This has all happened painlessly since Franklin Roosevelt's first administration through the application of the "golden rule." Under the golden rule, whoever has the gold, rules. And it is the federal government that can print money to finance any local activity from road building to school hot lunches. If the feds don't want us to drive faster than 55 m.p.h. in Wyoming or to drink below the age of twenty-one in New York, they need only tie the speed limit or drinking age to appropriations of federal highway funds and the states quickly pass accommodating statutes. The states are more interested in spending federal dollars than they are in preserving state sovereignty. To my knowledge no state (except, possibly, Arizona in one instance) has turned down federal money to stand on federalist principle! Therefore, if the states themselves aren't interested in principle, why should we be?

Furthermore, there is an understanding even among ordinary citizens of the problems inherent in fifty separate, sovereign, uncoordinated states. Thus, constituencies frequently repair to Congress to solve egregious problems that the states are incapable of solving. Although, as I said earlier, there is not sufficient consensus to enable Congress to fix the type of business problems that engage us here, there have been many interstate problems affecting broad constituencies that Congress has tried to solve through legislation. In recent years, family matters have figured prominently in this category.[1]

During the last two decades, as the divorce rate soared, both parental kidnapping and nonpayment of support became serious interstate problems. The lack of coordination among state courts, and the fact that state courts did not automatically accord full faith and credit to out-of-state custody decisions, made it profitable for a parent to kidnap his or her child and flee to another state where, conceivably, that parent had good political connections. Similarly, in an economy where over 34 percent of all previously married, female heads of household are on welfare, collecting child support and alimony from defaulting husbands across state lines, this has become a major social problem. A deadbeat husband living in Massachusetts can cause California to spend $8,000 a year supporting his wife and children, merely because they may happen to live in California.

Less than half of the women entitled to child support or alimony get anything, and of those who receive something, less than 30 percent receive it all. Although the solutions that Congress has devised for these problems aren't very effective, Congress has taken action in both areas. The *Parental Kidnapping Prevention Act* sets forth specific standards to be applied by state courts in cases of interstate child snatching, and the *Child Support Enforcement Act* has tied tighter enforcement of child support to federal welfare appropriations. (Another example of the "golden rule.") Yet both of these statutes would be much more effective if the federal courts would become interested in interstate family matters and provide some definite guidance concerning how these statutes should be interpreted and implemented.

Some of the state legislation designed to improve the collection

1. In earlier periods such things as antitrust, securities fraud, national unemployment insurance, and social security achieved high positions on the national legislative agenda. None of these latter subjects could have been handled by federal courts.

of interstate child support fails almost completely to accomplish the goals of Congress. There are at least two reasons for this failure. First, neither federal nor state legislators understand the mechanics of how courts work. Second, the child support statute offers endless pork-barrel opportunities at the state level for jobs. For example, West Virginia's efforts at compliance with the *Child Support Enforcement Act* involved the creation of thirty-five law masters to try divorce cases and enforce support awards. But West Virginia never had a problem getting divorces tried; our big problem was getting the papers drawn and served so indigent women could drag their deadbeat former husbands into court. Many of the upper-middle-class activists in the women's lobby saw in the law master program thirty-five quasi-judgeship appointments that would be available *to them*. But what West Virginia really needed was a few masters (to do nothing but enforce alimony and child support) combined with lots of legal aid lawyers to draw contempt-of-court papers to get defaulters into court, and lots of deputy sheriffs to serve the papers and arrest defaulters. All Congress and our state legislature did was fix something that wasn't broken, while failing to solve the real problem. That problem was lack of the free legal staff necessary to enforce small claims—a situation that was obvious to even the most pedestrian trial judge and every family law practitioner. But women political activists wanted jobs as judges and not jobs as legal aid lawyers or process servers.

The history of the *Child Support Enforcement Act* is eloquent testimony to the fact that, notwithstanding whatever theory of decentralized government prompted the original constitutional vision, all of the practical conditions that underlay that vision have changed so dramatically that historical federalism no longer makes any sense. Ordinary citizens, like divorced women with children, who find themselves the victims of the chaotic law of uncoordinated states, look to the national government for help.

There will inevitably be the legitimate objection from formalists that the *Constitution*—our supreme law—must be literally enforced until properly amended. But since the dawn of legal science honest lawyers have struggled with the problem of written laws that have not kept pace with changes in society, and with perfect integrity have developed principles for accommodating flexibility to the rule of written law. Perhaps the definitive statement on the subject may be found in Roman law in Book One of *The Digest of Justinian,* "De Legibus Senatusque Consultis Et Longa Constuetudine 32," where the following proposition is attributed to the praetor in the reign of Julian[2]:

> Age-encrusted custom is not undeservedly cherished as having almost statutory force, and this is the kind of law which is said to be established by use and wont. For given that statutes themselves are binding upon us for no other reason than that they have been accepted by the judgment of the populace, certainly it is fitting that what the populace has approved without any writing shall be binding upon everyone. What does it matter whether the people declares its will by voting or by the very substance of its actions? Accordingly, it is absolutely right to accept the point that statutes may be repealed not only by vote of the legislature but also by the silent agreement of everyone expressed through desuetude.

The second argument for federalism is what I call "result-oriented" federalism which, notwithstanding its disingenuousness, generates the most die-hard political support. Result-oriented federalism is based on the simple phenomenon that, because the controlling constituencies at the state level are different from the controlling constituencies at the national level, state governments and the federal government find different political solutions to the same political problems. When I was young the most prominent incarnation of result-oriented federalism went under the sobriquet "states' rights." If a person was unenthusiastic about racial integration, the rallying point was simply that race relations were a matter best left to the states. And, obviously, the political structure of the southern states was such that little integration was likely to occur during lives-in-being plus twenty-one years. In the 1960's, of course, the liberal wings of both parties laughed states' rights to scorn, but those same folks would probably voice "federalism" objections today to a national common law simply because national law administered by life-tenured federal judges might be more favorable to business than is current local law.

The idiocy of trying to make federalism into a useful concept

---

2. It is worth remembering that Julian reigned in the late fourth century when the Empire was very old. After more than 400 years of imperial history alone, Rome must have had an unbelievable body of obsolete law that had never been formally repealed but which was at odds with custom and usage in that age. For a good discussion of the general problem of obsolete statutes, see G. Calabresi, *A Common Law for the Age of Statutes* (Cambridge, Mass.: Harvard University Press, 1982).

in result-oriented debates can be seen from the vacillating positions that interest groups take on the subject simultaneously. For example, local governments lobby incessantly for more federal money for education. Yet local governments scream about a decisive blow to federalism when the Supreme Court rules that local government must pay the federal minimum wage to municipal transit company bus drivers. Similarly, the same plaintiffs' lawyers and criminal defense lawyers who have brought us racial integration, nondiscrimination in employment, civil rights, and civil liberties through federal court decisions using the Bill of Rights as the fulcrum, scream like stuck pigs when it is suggested that federal courts might intrude into commercial matters under the Constitution's commerce or equal protection clauses. Result-oriented federalism, then, is simply a matter of political muscle combined with some quick conclusions about whose ox is going to be gored. Although result-oriented federalism is of enormous practical concern, it is unworthy of being taken seriously in terms of legal principles.

However, the third argument for federalism—namely, practical federalism—is an argument worthy of the most serious and fastidious consideration. Many knowledgeable observers believe that much of America's efficiency, entrepreneurial dynamism, and upward mobility is directly related to the federal structure. Although it is impossible to summarize here all the practical arguments for federalism, the most important of them is that our federal structure inspires competition among *governments* in the same way that free enterprise inspires competition among private *businesses.*

Much recent economic literature points out that in every society political coalitions form for the purpose of affecting the distribution of wealth.[3] Mathematical models examining the logic of collective action demonstrate that distributional coalitions—such as labor unions, manufacturers' cartels, and populist political parties—are difficult to organize, but that once they are in place they are nearly impossible to dismantle. One (but only one) explanation for the remarkably unspectacular economic growth of Europe in general, and England in particular, in the last decade is that

3. See *e.g.,* M. Olson, *The Rise and Decline of Nations* (New Haven: Yale University Press, 1982).

distributional coalitions have significantly impaired business incentives and distorted efficient resource allocation.

According to Professor Mancur Olson, who has written exhaustively in this area,[4] one reason why both Germany and Japan experienced extraordinarily high rates of economic growth in the
1960's (after postwar rebuilding was complete) was not that the
war had destroyed their obsolete plants, but that the war had destroyed their distributional coalitions. Certainly history bears this
out. The primary occupying power in both West Germany and
Japan was the United States, and during the occupation we imposed American ways of doing things on both countries. Among
these American ways of doing things were broad-based industrial
unions, discouragement of cartels, universal suffrage, labor mobility, civil rights, and unbridled free enterprise. After formal occupation, however, distributional coalitions again developed and began to exert political power, but they have taken different forms
from what we currently see in England, France, and Sweden,
where distributional coalitions have enjoyed long, uninterrupted
historical evolutions.

This analysis becomes relevant to American federalism because
much of the current geographical shift in the center of the American economy from North to South, and from East to West, can be
explained in terms of flights from distributional coalitions. At the
simplest level there is a flight from traditionally unionized, high-
wage states like New York, Pennsylvania, and Michigan to traditionally low-wage, nonunionized states like South Carolina, Florida, and Arizona. But the distributional coalitions that individuals
can assemble for themselves—like labor unions, business cartels,
and professional associations—pale in comparison to the distributional coalitions that can be established through government.
Thus one strong argument for continuing a decentralized, federal
structure is that when the federal government in the United States
is a government of limited powers, it is state and local government
that must be importuned to translate political power into all the
various forms of wealth redistribution—ritualized job security,

4. *Ibid.* See also M. Olson, *The Logic of Collective Action,* revised edition (Cambridge, Mass.: Harvard University Press, 1971).

high wages unrelated to efficiency, social services, and social insurance.[5]

Part of our efficiency *vis-à-vis* England, France, and Sweden (to say nothing of the Soviet bloc, where most resource allocation is determined by political rather than market rules) is that in the United States state governments must compete with one another exactly as businesses must. Studies of both state and national legislative elections disclose that there is a significant correlation between the level of employment and whether a political party will remain in power.[6] Furthermore, the ability of state and local government to reward their supporters with jobs and contracts, and to deliver on their promises about social services and public works, is entirely dependent upon the tax base. When, therefore, both private job opportunities and the tax base are taken into consideration, distributional coalitions cannot extort the same concessions from the private sector in the United States that they can in European countries, because here the extortee businesses will vote against the extorting locale with their feet. The point is perhaps proven by the fact that in France the socialist government of François Mitterand had to place draconian restrictions on capital flight (and even private travel) in 1982 to avoid an unfavorable foot ballot after the inauguration of traditional socialist programs.

A good example of the distributional coalition problem can be seen in the different rates of job creation in Western Europe and the United States. Under the guise of social justice, West European

5. This is not to say, however, that all social programs designed to alleviate human suffering are necessarily foreclosed by the federal structure. Thus Title IX of the Social Security Act of 1935 (42 U.S.C. §1101) established a national system of employment security under which unemployed workers could receive state-administered unemployment compensation. The method used to achieve this desirable national goal was to impose a federal tax on employers (now levied under 26 U.S.C. §3301 *et seq.*) unless a state levied its own employment security tax to establish a state unemployment compensation system. If the states failed to act, the federal tax was simply paid into the Treasury without earmark, but if the states established qualifying state employment security systems, 90 percent of the state tax was a credit against the federal tax. Mr. Justice Cardozo pointed out in *Steward Machine Co. v. Davis*, 301 U.S. 548 (1937) that the purpose of the federal tax was to avoid differences in manufacturing costs among the states so that states would *not* be discouraged from inaugurating employment security programs from fear that their industries would be placed at a competitive disadvantage.

6. For a quick summary, see R. Neely, *How Courts Govern America* (New Haven: Yale University Press, 1981), p. 26, n. 2.

countries have created a two-tier economy that grants extensive protection to employed workers but makes it difficult for new workers to enter the labor market. A worker with a job in Western Europe enjoys great security and attractive wages, but there are few pressures to adjust wages and enhance job flexibility. In this regard, the British case is the paradigm. Despite an unemployment rate exceeding 12 percent, real per-capita earnings in Britain increased by roughly 3 percent between 1983 and 1985. In the first quarter of 1985, British labor costs jumped 6 percent!

During the 1970's the anti-growth effect of distributional coalitions in Europe was obscured by unemployment rates that were lower than in the United States. But what was really happening was that total employment was declining because prime-age male participation rates were falling, the foreign labor force was being repatriated, and female participation rates were increasing only slowly. Thus at the same time that America was creating millions of jobs—many for women and minorities—Western Europe had an absolute decline in employed workers.

Rigid dismissals legislation in European countries has transformed labor costs into fixed costs. When wage differentials were increasing between sectors of the economy in the United States and Japan from 1973 to 1982, they were narrowing in Western Europe, which meant that workers were not redirected from declining industries. Furthermore, in Europe there is more incentive than anywhere else in the world to substitute capital for labor. The distributional coalitions composed of *employed* workers who want high wages and strong security have created a rising relative cost of labor, and the rigid labor laws have discouraged the substitution of efficient workers for inefficient ones. At the same time, investment subsidies prompted by industry's political muscle have made investment in labor-saving equipment more attractive than investment in people.

But in the separate states of the United States, even the *threat* that segments of the job-creating private sector will flee across state lines (or even abroad) has an incalculable tempering effect on both the militancy and effectiveness of distributional coalitions. And ironically, at least from the European point of view, one of the functions of the national government that has unconsciously evolved here in the United States is the evisceration by the national government of distributional coalitions at the state and local level. At the simplest level, this has meant the intrusion of the federal government into race relations in the South to avoid allocations of economic benefits on the basis of color. At a slightly more complicated level, federal control of bankruptcy establishes a perimeter around the perennial battles between debtors and creditors, and creates a uniform national system that is resistant to anti-creditor, populist urges.

Much of the theory of the current federal-state balance proceeds directly from the wisdom of *Federalist* 10 (Madison), where it is pointed out that it is more unlikely that a faction (distributional coalition) will take control at the national level (where there are more balancing constituencies) than at the state level, where one narrow constituency (like farmers or industrial workers) can command a plurality. The genius of the federal structure, then, is that because most of the subjects that distributional coalitions wish to control (like job security) must be controlled at the state level, distributional coalitions are usually weak at the national level. But, precisely because the distributional coalitions are weak at the national level, it is often possible to use national law to weaken them even further when they attempt to dominate state and local government. This is the reverse of the classic vicious cycle; while the structural dynamics of centralized European countries tend to make distributional coalitions stronger and stronger, our dynamics tend to make them weaker and weaker. Thus the dramatic decline in unionized workers as a percentage of the labor force in the last decade.

Fortunately, any theory of federalism—historical, result-oriented, or practical—has inherent limits that can logically be found in the structure of the *Constitution of the United States* itself. Although the framers would not have expressed it this way, these limits proceed from the problem of "externalities." If either the benefits or the costs of a governmental action are experienced outside the jurisdiction where the action is taken, then it is logical to consign that issue to the national government. One instance of the problem of externalities specifically mentioned in the *Constitution* is defense. Were it not for the *Constitution*, Rhode Island could contribute nothing toward its own defense with impunity— just as Mexico contributes nothing to protect itself now—because states that choose not to pay their fair share for the defense of North America will still be protected by the states that choose to maintain military forces.

Modern life brings examples of externalities undreamt of by the founders, such as factories in one state that pollute the air and cause acid rain to fall on the forests of other states, or a dam constructed in one state that causes rivers to dry up in another.[7] The problem of externalities is at the heart of the competitive race to the bottom, and externalities are the justification for a federal common law. Even purist defenders of historical federalism concede that Congress can deal with the externalities problem; they begin to choke only when it is suggested that the courts can do it.

There is one final rationale for practical federalism that should be mentioned because it relates directly to the mechanics of how we implement a federal common law. This rationale is that small local government is more efficient than big national government. At the simplest level, getting a record from your local county courthouse is a surpassingly pleasant experience compared to getting a similar record from the Social Security Administration, although, like the county courthouse, Social Security has a local office nearly everywhere. Just within the last year I have discovered that the federal government has two record-processing centers—one a regional IRS office in Ohio, and the other an INS visa-processing center in Maine—that have *secret* telephone numbers. It is not just that the numbers are unlisted; it is apparently a high crime or misdemeanor for any government employee to disclose those numbers to anyone. Yet in state government you can get high-ranking department heads on the telephone within a few days. In a state as small as West Virginia, any ordinary citizen can get an appointment to see the governor within two weeks. During my terms as West Virginia's chief justice, I talk *personally* to every person who calls my office. In the federal government you can't even get through to a G.S. 7 IRS or INS records clerk, much less a cabinet officer or commissioner.

In large countries with centralized national governments the diseconomies of scale can be so acute as to be entirely laughable. In 1984 I spent a month teaching law at Fudan University in Shanghai, where the students in my seminars discussed the then-current Chinese government structure. It turns out that one of the primary uses of the Chinese civil court system is to sort out contract problems between work units that are within the same ministry. The bureaucracy is so top-heavy that it is easier to settle a

---

7. The classic treatment of externalities may be found in R. H. Coase, "The Problem of Social Cost," 3 *J. Law & Econ.* 1 (1960).

dispute between a bicycle manufacturer and a supplier of rubber tires about quantity, price, and delivery dates for tires in a court than it is to go up the chain of command to the person who is nominally the boss of both operations.

Both historical federalism and result-oriented federalism, if taken seriously, could present significant obstacles to the creation of a federal common law. Practical federalism, however, presents no obstacles. Certainly there is less reason to believe that a distributional coalition will capture the federal courts than there is to believe that distributional coalitions will capture state courts. Furthermore, there is no reason to believe that federal judges, as a class, will be either more or less disposed to plaintiffs on political or philosophical grounds than state court judges.[8] But federal courts will be able to control a sufficient number of variables so that they can balance competing national goals. Protection from accidents for individuals, wealth redistribution to random victims, and product safety are desirable social goals. But they are not free and someone must intelligently evaluate whether we can afford them. For example, I do not know the extent to which product liability law deters economic growth or product innovation because that is not a subject that is even casually briefed today in the state courts that consider product liability cases. The current system makes the issue entirely irrelevant, but that is a stupid way to govern a country.

It seems, at least to me, that the legal and political structure of America implies that federal common law is an appropriate, integral part of the federal government's job of reducing the burdensome effect of externalities on everyone's life. From a practical point of view there is little difference between the federal Congress undertaking to make sure that one state's industry doesn't pollute another state's air and the federal courts' undertaking to make sure that one state's law isn't set up to redistribute another state's wealth. When California and Texas simultaneously claimed Howard Hughes' estate taxes, no interest whatsoever was served

8. Although in many states judges are elected, those elections can be controlled either by populists or moneyed interests, depending on who happens to be interested at the time. When populists dominate a state court system for a while, the moneyed interests get their act together and get some judges elected through slick media campaigns. When the moneyed interests have dominated for a while, the populists get organized and win a few elections. Consequently, the process is similar to how presidents appoint federal judges—the Carter appointees were liberal, while the Reagan appointees are conservative.

(except federal court docket control) by not having the question of which state was Mr. Hughes' residence decided quickly and authoritatively.

The one objection to a federal common law that emerges from practical federalism is that the undertaking might create a bureaucratic brontosaurus in the federal courts. Yet experience from areas of the law where the federal courts have established guidelines to be applied by state courts indicates that state courts will cheerfully accept federal guidance. Judging is hard, demanding work, and whenever there is a simple, bright-line rule that courts can apply, the judge's job is easier. About ten years ago in West Virginia we simplified the rules governing child custody in divorce cases. Our supreme court deliberately rejected fashionable modern doctrine that promotes exhaustive expert psychological testimony about parents and children before awarding custody, and made the bright-line rule that young children will always be awarded to their "primary caretaker" if that parent is fit. For all practical purposes, in West Virginia "primary caretaker" is a sex-neutral way of spelling "mother," but there have been a few occasions when fathers have qualified as primary caretakers under our criteria.[9]

The point for our purposes here, however, is that our mechanical rules about custody removed a significant amount of our trial court judges' discretion in domestic matters. But instead of the judges' complaining that we had substituted mechanical rules for their own good judgment, they were universally enthusiastic about the new system. They found that the children benefited because custody decisions were made quickly and without embarrassing, traumatic, in-court and out-of-court examinations of children, and that the divorcing parties did not feel compelled to spend what little money they had on expensive lawsuits that simply led—after much grief—to an award to the primary caretaker anyway. Furthermore, because the law was suddenly very clear, an increasing number of domestic cases were settled, and fewer cases required in-court hearings.[10]

---

9. In a northeastern urban area with less traditional family patterns, fathers would qualify under our law as primary caretakers fairly frequently. In West Virginia, however, most of the child raising in the coal fields is done by mothers. It's tough to take care of a two-year-old when you work overtime on the cat-eye shift.

10. See R. Neely, "The Primary Caretaker Parent Rule: Child Custody and the Dynamics of Greed," 3 *Yale Law and Policy Review* 168 (1984).

If, therefore, state judges respond in their characteristic, cooperative way to the rules laid down by the U.S. Supreme Court, there will not be a need for a larger federal court bureaucracy. What there will be a need for, obviously, is a slight change in the mix of cases on which the Supreme Court and lower federal courts spend their time. But adjustment of the mix of issues upon which the Supreme Court focuses its attention has been a process that has gone on throughout our history. In fact, in all courts it can be seen that new, unsettled issues tend to be litigated extensively, while issues governed by well-established, bright-line rules tend to be settled privately. For example, in the early part of this century, tort and contract matters took up a far higher percentage of court time than they do today, but as the rules in those areas got settled, fewer cases came to court because in-court outcomes were predictable. Similarly, in the 1960's, when the Supreme Court changed our law of criminal procedure, the federal district courts devoted a high percentage of their time to reviewing state criminal convictions. But in 1976, after the new criminal law had been firmly established, the Supreme Court ordered the lower federal courts to withdraw from day-to-day review of state criminal trials. Now federal courts overrule state convictions only when the state proceedings have made a "mockery of justice," or the state court has explicitly misapplied a constitutional principle.

It took the federal courts about twelve years to overhaul criminal procedure in the United States, and that was a far more complicated and controversial undertaking than tinkering at interstate commercial matters. In order to achieve its criminal law and related civil rights agenda, the Supreme Court almost completely stopped taking appeals from lower courts in federal commercial cases—cases which had once occupied much of its docket. Commercial cases were simply replaced with criminal and civil rights cases that arose on new, unsettled legal frontiers. But the law in criminal and civil rights cases has now been settled well enough that it can be administered—except for the extraordinary case—by the lower courts.

A specialist in American legal history is likely to find my analysis of the need for a unifying federal common law laughable in its simplicity. The reason is that the relationship between state law and federal courts has been the subject of scholarship approaching in magnitude that to be found in the *Encyclopedia Britannica.* Furthermore, a significant portion of this scholarship has proceeded from America's greatest legal minds—judges like Story, Taney, Holmes, Brandeis, Stone, and Frankfurter, along with professors like Yale's Arthur Corbin and Harvard's Charles Warren.[11] Between 1842 and 1938 the federal courts adhered to the principle (first comprehensively enunciated in the case of *Swift v. Tyson*) that federal courts could apply a national common law independent of the decisional law (and even the statutory law) of the states to cases over which the federal courts had jurisdiction. This broad doctrine, which began as a benign attempt to create a national law of commercial transactions, ultimately turned the federal courts into the handmaidens of corporations. The *Swift* doctrine has come to be much reviled because, by 1920, the federal courts were seen as purposeful vindicators of business interests at the expense of workers, consumers, and government regulators. By the time of the Great Depression, federal judges appeared to many articulate New Dealers as the preeminent class enemy.

Perhaps one of the most horrible examples of the abuses to which federal common-law principles led during the *Swift* era is a case called *Black and White Taxicab v. Brown and Yellow Taxicab*, decided by the Supreme Court in 1928. Two taxi companies, both Kentucky corporations, were competitors at a railroad station in Bowling Green. Black and White made a contract with the railroad, which granted them a monopoly, although Kentucky statutory law prohibited contracts creating monopolies. To avoid Kentucky law, Black and White dissolved its corporation and reincorporated in Tennessee for the express purpose of creating federal diversity jurisdiction. Once in federal court, Black and White argued that Kentucky's statutes against monopoly could not apply to foreign corporations because they were governed by the law of the place of incorporation. Because Tennessee law had no prohibition against monopoly contracts, Black and White asked the lower court to ignore the Kentucky law and to enforce their contract under general principles of commercial law. The federal trial court accepted Black and White's argument and the Supreme Court affirmed.

Abuses such as the Black and White case were finally eliminated

---

11. I am indebted for much of what follows concerning the *Swift* and *Erie* debate to a superb work of legal history by Professor Tony Allan Freyer, *Forums of Order: The Federal Courts and Business in American History* (Greenwich, Conn.: JAI Press, 1979).

in 1938 during the New Deal, when the Supreme Court decided *Erie Railroad v. Tompkins.* It held that federal courts must apply the law of the states where they are sitting, including a state's decisional law. So far I have avoided entanglement in the *Swift/Erie* historical controversy because the mountain of scholarship on the subject is likely to distract us from a straightforward, practical approach to a comparatively simple problem. Nonetheless, it is now important to point out that suggesting that the federal courts attempt to control the chaos inherent in fifty-two competing state or state-like court systems is not new.

For approximately half of America's history the federal courts took an active position on behalf of interstate business and were willing to ignore both state statutory and decisional law to do so. Furthermore, it is interesting to remember that the federal courts tried to unify American law only fifty-three years after the *Constitution* was ratified. The federal courts were a more important unifying force then than they are now because Congress was even less active in tying the country together in the nineteenth century than it is today. The history of the era of *Swift v. Tyson* is instructive, but, in resurrecting the notion that in some areas of the law the federal courts should establish national standards, it is not necessary to resurrect all of the abuses of federal court power that plagued consumers, debtors, and workers during the *Swift* era.

To give a thumbnail sketch of how federal courts have approached the "uncommon law" problem, American legal history for our purposes can be divided into three broad eras: (1) pre-*Swift* (1789–1842); (2) *Swift* (1842–1938); and (3) post-*Erie* (1938–present). Throughout all of this history there has been the troublesome problem of Section 34 of the *Judiciary Act* of 1789, which created the first system of federal courts. Section 34, known as *"The Rules of Decision Act,"* provided: "That the laws of the several states, except where the Constitution, treaties, or statutes of the United States shall otherwise require or provide, shall be regarded as rules of decision in trials at common law in the courts of the United States in cases where they apply."[12]

---

12. This provision, as amended, is now codified as 28 U.S.C. § 1652 (1982). It was amended in 1948 to eliminate the distinction between suits at common law and equity and now reads: "The Laws of the Several States, except where the Constitution or treaties of the United States or Acts of Congress otherwise require or provide, shall be regarded as rules of decision in civil cases in the courts of the United States, in cases where they apply."

During the early years of the Republic—the pre-*Swift* years—*The Rules of Decision Act* was thought to impede federal court creation of stable, national law. I say "impede" advisedly, because it seems unlikely that the drafters of Section 34 understood exactly what the national economy would look like twenty years after its passage, or what the effect of chaotic local law would be on that national economy. To say that in the early nineteenth century local state law was "unsettled" would be a significant understatement. Furthermore, although in the early nineteenth century the American economy was growing by leaps and bounds, the underdeveloped condition of state law, plus the outright hostility of state legislatures and courts to interstate commerce, were constantly seen as impediments to even faster growth.

Some of the peculiar problems that existed in the early nineteenth century are illuminated by the specific facts that gave rise to the *Swift* case. *Swift* involved a wonderfully complicated set of commercial transactions centering in the speculative purchase of wilderness land in Maine. The principal players were two Maine speculators and some New York financiers. The speculators decided to sell the New Yorkers' land that they did not yet own, but intended to buy with the New Yorkers' money. The New Yorkers, on the other hand, thought the speculators owned the land. Some of the New Yorkers gave the speculators negotiable instruments instead of money to satisfy their investment obligations. George W. Tyson, a member of the New York group, "accepted" a bill of exchange in return for a six-month postponement in the payment of one of his installments on the land contract.

One of the Maine speculators then gave Tyson's note to Joseph Swift, a Maine banker, in satisfaction of a preexisting debt, but when Swift sought payment from Tyson, Tyson refused to pay on the grounds that his obligation was unenforceable because he had been induced to "accept" the bill by the land speculators' fraud. Swift sued Tyson in federal court in New York, and the central question was whether the case should be decided under the old New York law of contracts, or under the new law of negotiable instruments—as developed by English decisions of Lord Mansfield. If New York law applied, then the fraud that tainted the original acceptance of the bill would be a defense for Tyson. But if the emerging law of negotiable instruments applied, then Tyson must pay Swift, if Swift had accepted the instrument without notice of the fraud.

Today few law students (and even fewer practicing lawyers) have any idea what negotiable instruments are all about. Part of the reason is that in a world dominated by wire transfers, bank checks, Federal Express, and Mastercard, there is little need for complicated commercial paper. But in the early nineteenth century, when commerce was growing rapidly among regions separated by weeks or months of travel, bills of exchange, warehouse receipts, bills of lading, letters of credit, and negotiable notes played a central role in business. And, in addition, commercial paper expanded the money supply. In this regard it must be remembered that in the nineteenth century money was backed by gold, and gold was scarce. As any alumnus of Economics 101 remembers, $MV = PT$ (money times velocity equals prices times transactions). According to this basic economic principle, commercial expansion requires a gently rising money supply if prices are to remain stable. Negotiable instruments, like today's Mastercard, allowed the money supply to expand by creating private near-money that could be taken with almost as much confidence as gold. (Today the discount for Mastercard is 3.5 percent, about the same transactional cost as yesteryear's commercial paper.)

The problem, however, was that for negotiable instruments to work they had to be enforced with Rhadamanthine severity. Thus, regardless of any fraud or chicanery that might taint an original transaction, once a negotiable instrument was given, the maker and endorsers had to be liable to any "holder in due course" who, unaware of the taint, took the instrument in payment of a debt. (This is basically the rule employed today by Mastercard, American Express, and Visa: these credit cards are all like cash, and if a store rips off the cardholder, the cardholder's fight is with the store, and not with the credit card company.)

In the early nineteenth century state courts were less enthusiastic about the negotiability principle than the federal courts. Part of their lack of enthusiasm was pure provincialism—a desire to protect local debtors from foreign creditors—but another part was simply the primitive and confused condition of much state law. Many formalistic state judges believed it improper to import new English commercial law, created only in the 1780's, into their own states, because English common law had stopped being "received" in the early eighteenth century when the colonies set up their own legislatures. Thus, binding state decisional law was often at odds with the new law of negotiable instruments, because commercial cases in states like New York had been decided on seventeenth-century English contract law, and not the late eighteenth-century English negotiable instruments law. This, in fact, was the situation in New York when Swift brought his suit against Tyson in federal court.

It was from such a background, then, that in 1842 the Supreme Court decided in favor of the creditor Swift, and ruled that in federal court the federal judges should apply a federal common law regardless of the law of the state where the court was sitting. The explicit acceptance of this principle—particularly in the face of *The Rules of Decision Act*—is what made *Swift* a striking case, but in fact the federal courts had often quietly ignored state law in commercial cases arising before *Swift*.

The immediate effect of *Swift* was to give greater uniformity and stability to interstate commercial matters. During most of the nineteenth century the imaginations of state governments were remarkably fertile in producing schemes to protect local businesses against foreign competition and to enhance the position of local debtors at the expense of foreign creditors. *Swift* allowed the federal courts to temper these schemes and to encourage the development of a continent-wide common market. But the original *Swift* principle emerged in an era of *commerce* when most business was carried on by large general merchants servicing a predominantly agricultural economy. *Swift* ended by doing things never contemplated by the Supreme Court that decided it.

When, after the Civil War, America was transformed into an industrial economy dominated by enormous interstate corporations (of which the railroads were the most prominent examples), the *Swift* doctrine came to be less and less about national law uniformity in neutral areas like negotiable instruments and more and more about achieving specific, pro-business results. American corporation law creates the legal fiction that a corporation is a legal "person," which means that if a business is incorporated in Delaware, it is an out-of-state citizen for federal diversity jurisdiction everywhere else. Thus almost all large corporations were foreigners in the states where they did business, which meant that almost everything that concerned corporations was governed by federal rather than state courts. At the high point of the *Swift* doctrine the federal courts cavalierly disregarded state law and applied protective, pro-business principles. But the New Deal brought populist judges to the Supreme Court in the late 1930's, at which point *Swift* went down the tubes.

In 1938 the Supreme Court decided *Erie Railroad v. Tompkins*— a case far simpler to explain than *Swift*. Tompkins was a trespasser on the right-of-way of the Erie Railroad when one of its passing trains struck him with the open door of a car. Tompkins sued the railroad in federal court. On the basis of federal common law, the lower federal court held for Tompkins, but the Supreme Court reversed on the grounds that it was overruling *Swift*. The court held in *Erie* that the law of Pennsylvania must apply, and under that law there was no duty to trespassers. Thus ended the *Swift* era: the rule since *Erie* has been that in diversity cases it is the law of the state where the court is sitting (including that state's rules regarding conflicts of laws) that governs diversity cases in federal court.

For those familiar with the whole *Swift / Erie* problem, my proposal for a court-made national law may sound dangerously close to suggesting a return to the *Swift* era. Yet there is a significant difference between what I propose here and what occurred during *Swift*. That difference is that I do not advocate different rules for federal and state courts. As I said earlier, the model for a new common law for business is not the federal court / state court dichotomy of the *Swift* era, but rather the national law unification accomplished in criminal procedure, libel, and state taxation of interstate commerce. In the *Swift* system the federal courts assumed that interstate business would organize itself to get into federal court, just as the Black and White taxi company did in 1922. At that point the federal courts simply applied a federal law for business independent of state law, and if the state courts wished to follow federal precedent (as they often did) then so much the better.

But in the model I propose the federal courts will not disturb the general rule of *Erie*. Routine business problems will still be settled under state law. Only in those areas like product liability, conflicts of law, interstate family matters, and competitive state jurisdictional fights will the federal courts impose a unified standard to be applied by all courts, state and federal.

The inevitable question, of course, is where to draw the line between those issues that require national standards and those that don't. The answer is that only those issues that present competitive race-to-the-bottom problems, or problems like Howard Hughes' residency, need to be dealt with by national law. Consequently, there is little reason to apply a federal standard in areas like contract law because most contract disputes arise between residents of the same state. Because the state court rules governing contracts have been crafted in intrastate settings, they have no inherent bias against out-of-state litigants. Product liability law, on the other hand, has a severe bias against out-of-state defendants because it has developed in a predominantly interstate setting.

At the high point of *Swift* there were approximately twenty-six areas of law that were governed by federal court rules. An exact listing is difficult here because they involve numerous technical and procedural distinctions, but the more important ones are: torts, particularly fellow servant issues; commercial law, particularly bonds, negotiable instruments, fiduciary liabilities, and insurance policies; wills; and property, particularly riparian rights. Today, many of the thorny areas of commercial law that engaged the federal courts during the nineteenth century are covered by uniform acts passed by most or all state legislatures. Preeminent among these is the *Uniform Commercial Code,* which attempts to unify the law of sales, commercial contracts, and negotiable instruments.

Finally, it is probably worth reciting the obvious—namely, that America at the end of the twentieth century is a different country from America in the middle of the nineteenth. Today, state government is both less parochial and more competent than it was then. When, for example, I was first elected to the West Virginia Supreme Court of Appeals, it was under a nineteenth-century state constitution that did not require the judges of our highest court to be lawyers. Today such judges must be lawyers with at least ten years of practice. Consequently, the task before us now does not involve dwelling on the problems of federalism in the nineteenth century, but rather imagining federalism in the twenty-first century. As administrative units, the states have proved highly successful, and federalism as a practical principle has proved remarkably resilient. Yet in many areas lack of coordination, and the competitive race to the bottom, plague the legal structure.

Whatever else can be said about the federal courts of the nineteenth century, they were at least visionary: they translated into law their perceptions of what would make America grow and prosper. But the type of intrusion by a uniquely scholarly, federal elite that was justified in the nineteenth century is no longer justified. Now state courts understand as well as federal courts that interstate business is the wellspring of job opportunities and tax bases. Furthermore, federal regulation of banks, the federal Bankruptcy Act, and the federal government's ability to expand the currency and apply Keynesian (and deficit) economics have all helped make the nineteenth-century battles between eastern commercial and industrial interests and western / southern debtor and farmer interests a thing of the past.

Policymaking appellate courts, like all other government policy-makers, have limited resources. This, then, necessarily implies that they must have agendas. When we are talking about a common law for business, the problem is not the crowded nature of the Supreme Court's docket in the abstract but simply that the issue of national law has not made the Supreme Court's current agenda. The Supreme Court's docket will always be crowded, but historically the Court has made room for those cases that present issues on its agenda. The trick, then, is not to worry about the docket but to concentrate on the agenda. Fortunately, the history of *Swift* implies that this issue can both make the agenda and occupy a reasonably high place on it.

Chapter 6

Judges as Political Hacks

Next to inheriting a personal fortune, a law degree is the surest ticket to a political career. Of West Virginia's six-person congressional delegation, four are lawyers. Although this ratio may be slightly higher than it is in other states, the most frequently recurring credential among ranking elected and appointed politicians—congressmen, senators, cabinet officers, governors, and senior bureaucrats—is a law degree.

Aside from the fact that going to law school is good training for government service, there are two other reasons why lawyers gravitate to government. First, young people who want political careers usually choose law school over other available graduate programs because they believe that a law degree offers income insurance against political losses. Second, law practice is a flexible career that allows a person to move in and out of government without taking a financial beating. In fact, intermittent government service can be a positive feature on a lawyer's resume: it proves that he knows about the operations of government from the inside. Government service also gives a lawyer friends and contacts that can be sold to clients for handsome fees.

Consequently, among any bar there are a sizable number of lawyers with political experience. Some of these lawyers have actually held high elective or appointed offices, but many others have simply been fund raisers or behind-the-scenes helpers of prominent politicians. Often this latter activity proceeds more from professional necessity than from the love of political life or dedication to a particular party. Law practice involves getting the government to do things for clients; a politician whose goodwill has been cultivated is more likely to return political favors. For a lawyer, one of the choice rewards for a lifetime of political participation is a judgeship. Often, indeed, a judgeship is the premier consolation prize for the also-rans of big-time elected politics. Earl Warren, for example, did not set out to be Chief Justice of the United States; he set out to be president.

In my own case, I went to the judiciary simply because, when I was thirty years old, it was the best political job I could get. In fact, I never wanted to be a judge at all; I wanted to be a United States Senator. I actually announced my candidacy for the U.S. Senate in 1971 and engaged in a six-month exploratory campaign in the hope that the incumbent would decide to retire. If he didn't retire, I hoped to beat him. Unfortunately for me, neither of these happy events occurred; the incumbent announced for reelection, and, at that point, most of my support—along with all of my money—dried up. Nonetheless, my luck was not entirely bad; in 1972 bad health and the Grim Reaper created two vacant seats on the elected West Virginia Supreme Court of Appeals. Because I had recently been in the state legislature and had inherited political support and name recognition from my grandfather, I thought I could capture one of those seats.

The voters were happy to elect a well-educated young man from an old political family to the low-visibility state supreme court because the voters thought of the court as a good entry-level job in statewide politics. The truth of the matter was that nobody cared much about the state supreme court, which was exactly the way I wanted it. It was thus a high tolerance for rubber chicken, and not a delicate mastery of the *Federalist Papers,* that got me a seat on West Virginia's highest court. Except for an occasional legal job in the army (where I was an artillery captain) I had practiced law for exactly three and a half years, and most of that time had been devoted to political campaigns or service in the legislature. To the extent that I have learned any law since law school, I have picked it up on the bench.

This short personal sojourn is simply to set the stage for a realistic discussion of how judges think and act. When I talk about judges' being a peculiar species of political hack, I am being autobiographical rather than critical. Much of the power of the judiciary is based on the decorum and solemnity of the institution: the black robes; the formality of the proceedings; and the obscurity of the language—including lingering passages from Latin—all serve to create the impression that judges are applying preconceived, scientific principles. The black robes make judges look like priests, which (from the point of view of staging) is probably better than dressing them like Boss Tweed. Nonetheless, robes and Latin notwithstanding, these guys and gals are just a bunch of politicians who spend all day running a big chunk of America's government.[1]

The nature of the judicial institution does prevent judges from sharing many of the vices of ordinary political hacks. All federal judges and many state judges have life tenure (and many other state judges have something close to life tenure), which means that there is little incentive for them to make meretricious political deals. High-level judges are infrequently involved in hardball partisan politics, and because of the limited size of the judiciary, judges are also seldom involved in turf wars or bureaucratic infighting. The ceremony that surrounds the presentation of a case to a court, and the elaborate and carefully enforced canons of judicial ethics, give judges a higher reputation for personal honesty and integrity than any of our other political actors. Although judges are often not impartial, or even knowledgeable about the law, it is a rare judge who is caught with his hand in the cookie jar.

A quick look at the backgrounds of U.S. Supreme Court justices and federal appeals court judges will disclose very few scholars. Today there is only one former law professor—Mr. Justice Scalia—on the U.S. Supreme Court, and fewer than 10 percent of federal circuit court judges come from academic backgrounds. This is not to say that the nonacademic judges aren't smart; it is only to say that their backgrounds have exposed them more to life's practical problems than to ivory-tower law school theory. The academic component in published court decisions comes predominantly from the battery of law clerks that are assigned to each justice or judge. A U.S. Supreme Court clerkship is almost a *sine qua non* for becoming a classy law professor. Judges tend to decide cases based on bottom line political results (using "political" in the best sense

---

1. I have always thought that in the costuming business the English are more colorful, as well as more honest, than we are. In the trial and appellate courts of England the costuming gets progressively more elaborate as we move from magistrate to high court judge to court of appeals judge. But once a litigant enters the land of the Law Lords, the highest court in the British Empire, we find the Law Lords dressed in ordinary business suits holding their hearings in a committee room of Parliament!

of the word), while the law clerks are expected to put the whole matter in proper academic form.[2]

In my experience, one of the major problems with the current legal process is that, because of the separation of the decision function from the explanation function, published opinions get farther and farther away from explaining the practical political reasons for the decisions. Nonetheless, as new cases arise, the arguments in those cases must still be couched in terms of the last published opinion touching the subject. Artificial academic reasoning, rather than practical politics, figures preeminently in most important court opinions because law professors are the primary audience for court opinions. Law is so boring that the popular press infrequently reports anything but the court's bottom line result. Minute dissection and heated criticism of court opinions come only from academia, where every professional lickspittle is in the business of proving that he is smarter and better educated than the Chief Justice of the United States. Many judges respond to law school and law review criticism by trying to head the professors off at the pass. At heart, the game usually amounts to a competition between judges' clerks and professors' student assistants.

The way things got this way goes back to black robes, Latin, and ceremony. It is a rare judge who is willing to say: "I'm a political hack and I decide all these issues pragmatically, one at a time." Part of the illusion of the "rule of law" is that everything is governed by general principles. And, in fact, everything *is* governed by general principles, but there are so many exceptions to the principles, and so many conflicting general principles, that the "general" concepts can be manipulated to achieve just about any desired result.[3] For example, in the United States the general rule is that in a lawsuit each side pays its own attorney's fees, win, lose,

2. Obviously this is a gross generalization and as such does not apply to all judges, or even to most judges all of the time. Many judges have gone to highly academic law schools from which they entered the practical world where they remained for decades. Once appointed to the bench, however, they often resurrect their earlier academic interests and become seriously involved in theoretical questions. Yet given the other demands on their time, even when judges want to be deeply involved in writing cases, they must still delegate much of their work if the court is not to become hopelessly backlogged.

3. In fact, this is exactly what happened to Texaco in the Texas Court of Appeals opinion. The court so manipulated general legal principles that they figured out a way to convert press releases into contracts and agreements to agree into ironclad, binding obligations.

or draw. But in the *U.S. Code* alone there are more than fifty separate fee-shifting statutes shifting litigation costs to a losing deep
pocket, and in the statutes and decisional law of the states there
are even more exceptions to the general rule on attorneys' fees.
One exception that often emerges at the state level from a combination of court decisions and general insurance statutes is that
when an insured must sue his own insurer over first-party insurance and wins, the insurer must pay reasonable attorneys' fees because of the statutory obligation to settle insurance claims in
"good faith." The net result of all this is that by now there is a
sufficient body of statutory and decisional law out there on fee
shifting, so that good lawyers can almost always piece together
some plausible argument that will justify shifting litigation costs
to the deep pocket defendant. Whether, therefore, the fee will be
shifted in any given case is often a hit-or-miss matter.

There are good historical reasons for the way law has come to
be expressed. Up until the twentieth century people tended to go
to court time and time again over the same types of disputes: property disputes, family disputes, contract disputes, inheritance
rights, and personal injuries tended to repeat common factual patterns. Because the factual patterns recurred with such frequency
in a society that changed little from decade to decade, looking at
how the issue was decided before gave significant guidance as to
how it should be decided again. But this was long before the center
of political power began to shift in the direction of the courts.

There are still routine issues that can properly be controlled by
precedent, but how does traditional contract law help us decide
the appropriate standards to apply to disputes about credit cards?
Credit cards are no longer a luxury for a small group of middle-
class business travelers: without a credit card, a traveler is a non-
person. Hotels require credit card identification for check-in; car
hire companies won't rent a car to a driver without a credit card;
and shopping by 800 telephone number through the catalogues is
nearly foreclosed without a credit card. The principles that bear
upon the rights of a credit card company and one of its cardholders in the event of a "wrongful" cancellation (however we define
"wrongful") are not illuminated by traditional contract or commercial law principles. Because of the extent to which commercial
institutions have shaped themselves around credit cards, credit
card companies have some obligation to provide reasonable access
to these cards. Both barriers to entry and economies of scale make

the credit card industry highly concentrated. Cases involving credit cards, therefore, must be decided by looking at the overall commercial system. Credit card companies, obviously, can't be compelled to give cards to deadbeats time and time again, but they also cannot be allowed to pick and choose arbitrarily those with whom they will do business. The standards that apply to a bank when it declines to make a private loan are not necessarily the appropriate standards to apply to a bank credit card franchisee when it declines to issue a credit card.

With the exception of the simplest, recurring legal problems, there is no single, correct way to decide any particular legal matter. Complicated legal matters, like the rights of cardholders *vis-à-vis* credit card companies, are simply political issues that have been consigned to courts rather than to the other branches of government for solution. In this regard the powers of the courts are usually residual: issues that are of enormous importance to only small groups at any one time tend to be decided by courts because the concerned constituency is not sufficiently large or well organized to place the issue on the legislative agenda. History is a good guide to the extent to which the division between judicial matters and legislative matters is fairly arbitrary. For example, it is only in the last hundred years that judges have been authorized to grant divorces; before that, divorces were granted by acts of the legislature.

Many cases that reach senior appellate courts today involve such broadly political issues as the appropriate trade-off between economic growth and employee security; the proper balance between debtor and creditor interests; the value of predictability in commercial matters *versus* fairness in particular cases; and consumers' interest in cheap, affordable products *versus* the consumers' interest in product safety. Underlying many of the issues that come before courts are questions concerning the proper distribution of wealth and power in American society. How these matters are decided has a lot to do with the background, education, and political convictions of judges.

In the universe of practical judges sitting on high-level appellate courts, there are subsets of judges of every possible political persuasion. Thus we often have free marketeers, New Dealers, closet socialists, civil libertarians, male chauvinist pigs, traditional moralists, and radical feminists all serving on the same court. And even within each broad subset, each individual judge has his or her own peculiar vision of what the social contract is all about. Thus, notwithstanding the academic game played by talented law clerks, it is ultimately each judge's underlying vision of the ideally just social contract that instructs that judge's understanding of important cases. Precedent and the lawyers' skillful manipulation of conflicting general principles take a back seat in the ultimate decision-making process to any judge's internally generated view of "just" relations among people.

Perhaps the difference between good judges and bad judges is not the presence or absence of preconceived notions of the proper social contract, but rather the presence or absence of a willingness to listen open-mindedly to other points of view. In my experience, good judges are characterized by an open-mindedness that allows preconceived notions to be refuted by facts. Most judges of my acquaintance generally agree with this view of the difference between good judges and bad judges, and of those who agree, all would prefer to be good judges rather than bad ones. There are, of course, some elected state judges who believe—often correctly—that their job security depends upon satisfying a particular electoral constituency that delivers campaign money and election-day votes. Also among appointed judges there are many who value ideological consistency above every other consideration.

On balance, however, a majority of judges try to be open-minded in terms of the most practical way to achieve their vision of the just social contract. Thus, a judge who is a die-hard free marketeer may still favor affirmative action for blacks to overcome centuries of discrimination. His free-market philosophy is broad enough to recognize a need to put blacks in a position where they can compete in a free market. On the other hand, a radically liberal black judge may be willing to narrow affirmative action law. He may conclude that affirmative action is appropriate in the hiring process, but that forcing employers to retain or promote minority workers who perform poorly may subtly discourage minority hirings. Thus, two judges with diametrically opposite political philosophies could agree on a specific policy concerning affirmative action. The judge who dislikes state action in principle may be willing to accept it as a stopgap measure, and the judge who believes in state action in principle may be willing to limit its use because it doesn't achieve the desired result. Both judges, then, could agree that affirmative action should be aggressively enforced at the hiring stage, but that once hired, an employee should have a very heavy burden to establish a case of discriminatory discharge.

The individual judge's view of the social contract, however, is still the key to his or her decisions. For example, let us imagine a case where a woman shoe store clerk in a small shoe store is fired because she is pregnant and she sues her employer for sex discrimination. The law provides that discharge for pregnancy *alone* is sex discrimination. The facts clearly disclose that there are but two things that a shoe store clerk does in a small shoe store: (1) get shoes down from high shelves; and (2) try those shoes on customers' feet. The facts also show that the employer kept the employee as long as possible, but finally became anxious that she would injure herself and her unborn child by falling from the ladder while fetching shoes. Such an injury would be chargeable to the employer under workers' compensation. Furthermore, the customers were embarrassed by the obvious strain involved in the clerk's bending over their feet in her pregnant condition to fit the shoes. Yet there was no question that the clerk was performing her job competently and without complaint—the embarrassment of the customers was entirely subjective. Who should win?

The answer, of course, depends upon how one answers the question: "Was she fired for pregnancy *alone*?" A judge whose view of the social contract values the rights of private property and freedom of contract for their own sakes, and who sympathizes with the problems of employers, is likely to conclude that, although the customers' embarrassment was irrational, their embarrassment was a significant business problem for the employer. Embarrassment, though irrational, inspired customers to leave before buying a pair of shoes. Yet, if a judge's view of the social contract is that the most important values to be advanced by the court-made law are job security and the narrowing of wealth differences, that judge will be reluctant to believe that there was no alternative to firing the employee. That judge, then, will decide the case for the employee. It is, therefore, the judge's view of the social contract, rather than ambiguous principles of law, that provides the organizing principle by which the facts in any specific case are catalogued and analyzed.

The pregnant shoe clerk's case is a real case, and it was decided by our court in favor of the clerk by a 3 to 2 decision. Unfortunately for business, "legislative" facts that might have changed the mind of one of the majority justices were never presented to the court.[4] What happens, for example, to the job prospects of unskilled women of childbearing age if pregnant workers cannot be fired? The answer, probably, is that young women will have a harder time getting a job in the first place. When an employer has five applications for one position, it is difficult to prove that he hired a thirty-five-year-old woman over a twenty-year-old woman simply because the former wouldn't get pregnant. Even a judge unsympathetic to employers might be willing to trade a small amount of job security in exchange for enhanced employment opportunities for younger, entry-level women.

Both my hypothetical discussion of how judges might approach affirmative action, and the real shoe store case, are examples of the interplay between legislative facts and judicial philosophy. But it should be obvious in the examples I have given that the important "facts" are not the "facts" of the particular case, but rather the broader "facts" of what will happen to different groups under alternative legal rules. The "fact" that is probably most relevant to the decision of the shoe store case has nothing whatsoever to do with what occurred in the store: the important "fact" involves the effect of alternative decisions on the employment opportunities for unskilled women of childbearing age.

Courts, as we all know, make every bit as much law as legislatures. When we put together the courts' power to develop common law and their power to interpret constitutions and statutes, the degree to which our everyday lives are governed by the policy choices of judges, rather than those of legislators, becomes painfully obvious. The shoe store case is a good example: determining that it is illegal to discharge a woman because she is pregnant is a long way from the explicit wording of the federal and state civil rights statutes that prohibit discrimination on the basis of sex. To those uninitiated into the arcana of legal reasoning, firing a pregnant woman and hiring another woman would not appear to be discrimination based on sex.

4. The term "legislative facts" is the invention of political scientists, and refers to the type of considerations, in the context of precedent-shattering lawsuits, that would be of interest to legislators if they were deciding the same issues. Legislative facts differ from the specific facts of the lawsuit in that they have nothing to do with the specific actions of the parties to the suit. Rather, legislative facts relate to the society-wide effect of one rule of law as opposed to its alternative.

The irony of the lawmaking power of courts is that it has been denied by so many for so long that court procedures are not set up to perform the lawmaking function particularly well. The eighth-grade civics class model of the political world consigns lawmaking to legislatures, and the application of the laws to the courts: usually, when politicians or laymen remark that the courts are legislating, the observation is condemnatory. Consequently, even obscenely activist judges prefer their lawmaking to proceed under cover of interpreting existing laws. Seldom is there an explicit recognition that courts are singlehandedly revolutionizing human relations.

And, of course, in terms of percentages of judicial time, most of what courts do is to apply existing law to pedestrian cases. Unfortunately, however, the procedures that efficiently dispatch the routine business of the courts are entirely inappropriate to the task of creating new law. When, for example, we talk about a wholesale reform of product liability law, precedent helps us very little. After all, it is existing precedent that we seek to reform. What really instructs our understanding of what the law *ought* to be are sociology, economics, political philosophy, and even engineering. Yet in the court process policy considerations are seldom discussed in these terms. Ironically, the formalities and ceremony surrounding all judicial proceedings, and the artificial language of precedent through which issues are presented to courts, guarantee that policymaking judges will be the most ignorant of all the major actors in the political process.

It is infrequently that I have any reason to call a justice of the U.S. Supreme Court, but on those rare occasions when I have called, I have spoken to the justice at once. The reason is not that I am an especially important person, or that my concerns enjoy public urgency. Rather, the reason that I get through so quickly is that Supreme Court justices don't do anything all day long but sit in their offices, talk to their law clerks, and think about their cases. Deciding important cases is difficult and serious work, but it is carried on in surpassing quiet and solitude. Although Supreme Court justices probably have more power per person than anyone in government except the president, it is easier to get a Supreme Court justice on the phone than it is the lowliest freshman member of Congress. The availability of Supreme Court justices is a function of their isolation, and their isolation is the product of the formality and ceremony of court processes.

No one with any business before the U.S. Supreme Court may talk to a judge about that business outside of the formal sittings of the Court. A Congressman, on the other hand, is deluged with importunings from every outraged constituent, special-interest-group spokesperson, and freelance proponent of good government who can find him in his office, at home, or even in a public men's room. In fact, the essence of the elected political function is accessibility to constituents: the essence of the judicial function, however, is withdrawal and separation. It is important to understand, therefore, the crucial distinction between elected legislators and policymaking appellate judges: legislators are *involuntary* consumers of information, while appellate judges are *voluntary* consumers of information. The conventions that circumscribe judges' activities are designed to enhance integrity, but they do so at the price of information.

The contrast between the way in which legislators and judges acquire information becomes important when we think about the need for legislative facts. When I was a member of a state legislature, I found it difficult to get any time for myself. In the evening, when I returned to my hotel from the state capitol, I usually entered by going down a back alley, wended my way through the garbage cans and accumulated deliveries at the service entrance, took the service elevator to the tenth floor, and sprinted up the stairs to my top floor room. Going through the formal lobby invited lengthy conversations with lobbyists, constituents, citizen groups worried about sex education in the public schools, and near-homicidal environmentalists. As a legislator, my mail often contained more than fifty letters a day that demanded sufficient thought to require a personally dictated reply, and the telephone rang off the hook whenever I was at home between sessions. Furthermore, campaigning for office demanded that I attend every imaginable function from Rotary Club luncheons to Polish weddings. On these stimulating occasions everyone with any conceivable bitch about government felt free to unload on me. Now, however, like my betters on the U.S. Supreme Court, I can sit for days at a time without a telephone call from anyone but my wife, and without a letter of more pressing concern than a request to save the whales.

Fully 95 percent of everything I heard as a legislator was unstructured background noise, but the remaining 5 percent was real information that provided me with necessary legislative facts to

perform my official duties. For example, in order to evaluate proposed legislation that would regulate stripmining, I thought it important to visit stripmines and observe their operation. Yet there
was also a personal political advantage incidental to gathering
such information: the very process of information-gathering
brings politicians into contact with voters under the most favorable possible conditions. When you visit a stripmine you have an
opportunity to shake hands with all of the miners, exchange a few
pleasant words, and at the same time hit the management up for
a campaign contribution for the next election.

On one occasion I was chairman of a subcommittee evaluating
alternative plans for a new mental health facility. In 1971 mental
health was a hot topic in West Virginia because our most important state hospital had been built before the Civil War. There were
several possible approaches to the mental health problem, each
advocated by a different group of health care professionals. To
reconcile the differences and arrive at a compromise plan, I held
an open subcommittee meeting in my hotel suite; the meeting began in the early evening and went on until 5:00 a.m. the next
morning, with all of the representative experts in attendance. The
result was a compromise that everyone felt comfortable supporting. I probably enjoyed that particular subcommittee assignment
more than anything else I did in the legislature, but I was also
aware that involvement in mental health generates goodwill from
a lot of ordinary voters who are otherwise quite indifferent to politics of any kind.

Thus legislators garner significant personal benefits from the
process of information-gathering, but a judge who is too curious
about the real world may even be punished. In the spring of 1986
our court had a case before it between the United Mine Workers
and various coal operators concerning mine safety standards in
low seam coal. About a month before the case arrived in our court
I had promised my five-year-old son that I would take him to visit
a real coal mine. I even went so far as to ask the executive director
of the West Virginia Coal Association to arrange a guided tour,
but when the mine safety case arose I canceled the trip. Had I
taken my son to the coal mine there might have been shrill criticism that I was allowing myself to be lobbied by the coal operators
without balancing input from the union. Had I gone and received
input from both sides, such a well-balanced tour would have de-

stroyed my primary purpose—namely, spending a day with my son in a real coal mine.

Judges can afford to be indifferent to the need for information because they enjoy perfect security. Legislators, on the other hand, must be sponges for information, because campaigning is inherently an information-gathering exercise. While legislators must smilingly and attentively sit through endless hours of unstructured background noise—and in the process uncover a few nuggets of valuable information—policymaking appellate judges don't need to listen to anything. Of course, court cases are allocated a certain time for oral arguments—usually half an hour for each side—but that is hardly an occasion that allows for the presentation of in-depth background information. To the extent that litigants want to submit detailed background information, that information must be provided in written briefs that are passed in great piles to members of the court. Do members of the court take these briefs home on Monday night to pore over them for endless hours, in preparation for the week's argument? Or do judges quietly close the doors to their studies and turn on the game? The answer, of course, is that some judges read the briefs; but a hell of a lot more watch the game. With the number of law clerks now available to every appellate judge, no judge ever *has* to read *anything*. This means, of course, that unlike politicians, an appellate judge's policy decisions may be instructed entirely by his or her own internally generated view of the world, based upon his or her limited personal experience.

The problem of lack of aggressive information-gathering by judges is exacerbated by the artificial language of the law. Next to the clergy, the legal profession has the longest uninterrupted history of all our social institutions, and many of its ways of doing things are historically given rather than consciously designed. We have had thousands of judges turning out opinions every year for hundreds of years. This means that there is at least some precedent for just about any proposition, no matter how absurd. There are, of course, many areas of the law where the weight of authority so strongly favors one outcome over other possibilities that we can say that the law is clear. However, those are not the cases that interest us in this book: in American law, for example, there is ample *precedent* both for and against a national common law.

The era of *Swift v. Tyson,* when the Supreme Court tried to estab-

lish a separate federal common law for interstate business, produced mountains of federal decisional law that is no longer good
precedent simply because the U.S. Supreme Court said so in *Erie
v. Tompkins.* But as every freshman law student knows, *Erie* can be
overruled by five Supreme Court votes, and the principles of *Swift*
resuscitated just as quickly as they were extinguished by *Erie.* Except in those few areas where the weight of authority overwhelm-
ingly favors one outcome, arguing from precedent is unpersuasive
at best, and distracting at worst. When deciding whether to accept
or reject new legal rules, what judges need to know are legislative
facts. And, regardless of whether the lawyers present their cases in
terms of legislative facts, the judges will decide important cases
based on what judges *believe* the legislative facts to be—notwithstanding that this belief may be based upon pure fantasy or political wishful thinking. In the case of the pregnant shoe clerk, my
own vote in favor of the employer was as ill-informed by any presentation of scientifically gathered legislative facts as those of my
colleagues who voted for the employee.

Earlier I observed that if lawyers bring enough cases to the U.S.
Supreme Court raising the issue of law unification, the Supreme
Court eventually will let a case in and think about the problem.
Unfortunately, however, there is more to a law unification campaign than simply filing traditional briefs that attempt to use precedent as a springboard to a new national common law. The tradi-
tion of state control of interstate tort claims, initiated by *Erie,* is
too well established to be put to rout without extensive preliminary political spadework. Before the bureaucracy of the U.S. Supreme Court will undertake a major transformation in American
law, there must be a clear showing that we have a serious problem
under the current system, and that the solution, national standards, will not be worse than the problem.

I use the term "bureaucracy of the U.S. Supreme Court" advisedly, because there are more than nine policymakers on the U.S.
Supreme Court. All but one of the Supreme Court justices have at
least three law clerks, and many have four. The chief justice has
court administrators and research assistants directly under his
control, and the Court itself has well-trained central staff lawyers
working in the clerk's office and in the library. The justices' personal law clerks are among the smartest and best-trained recent
law school graduates, and most of those clerks have had at least
one year of experience as law clerks on lower federal courts. The

individuals who comprise the Supreme Court's organized collective intelligence interact with one another in diverse ways (often, if rumor be credited, in very hostile ways), and it is this bureaucracy that is the primary conduit of information to the justices. Consequently, it is not essential in the first instance that the justices themselves be convinced that the Court should take a new look at law unification; it is sufficient that the law clerks and other central staff personnel be convinced that the Court should take a new look at law unification.

Happily for any business-sponsored, practical battle strategy, a majority of the Supreme Court's clerks traditionally go to law school teaching jobs rather than into active law practice. It is professionally important to these embryonic law professors that some earth-shattering decisions be made during their tenures as clerks. The fields of racial integration, civil rights, and criminal law have been so thoroughly ploughed that they are now unattractive areas to which to devote time and attention. This means that little is left for spectacular breakthrough except innovation in commercial law.

The problem, however, is that the creative opportunities offered by a new, national common law must be pointed out to aspiring academicians, and that requires a triumph in the art of propaganda. Propaganda always implies a certain deliberate but unrealistic simplicity, and although propaganda is anathema to serious thinkers, it has enormous value in any real political campaign. If all the theoretical issues that law unification will ultimately raise cannot somehow be contained, the practical political campaign will degenerate into incomprehensible law review articles that will bore everyone beyond tears. The problems created by the competitive race to the bottom, and by inconsistent rulings by uncoordinated state courts, are comparatively straightforward. Consequently those problems should be hammered home time and time again to the exclusion of everything else. Although the practical engineering will be difficult, the first priority is to develop a commitment to the project. In this regard reforming product liability law is like the Strategic Defense Initiative: The first step is a decision to try to do it, and the second step is to slog through the engineering problems.

It is business, of course, that has the most to gain by law unification, and happily business also has enough resources that it can explain the need for uniform law. Furthermore, it is highly fortunate for our efforts to reform product liability law that there are countless ordinary working Americans (like Mrs. Berger) who can understand the problem because of their own experience in divorce courts. These potential allies can provide valuable popular support if properly organized and led. In the last twenty years literally millions of people have taken beatings in interstate family squabbles where (notwithstanding the recent federal statutes), the state courts have served them up big helpings of home cooking. The National Organization for Women and the Women's Legal Defense Fund are not usually considered likely bedfellows for the National Chamber of Commerce, but in this area of concern the interests of NOW and the Women's Legal Defense Fund are identical to the interests of manufacturers and retailers who are hit by product liability suits. It is for this reason that I have presented the uncommon law problem in terms of the general case as well as in terms of the more specific problem of product liability.

The major obstacle to any law unification project, of course, is the inability of any one litigant to afford the propaganda effort necessary to put law unification on the Supreme Court's agenda just to win one case. In order to make the Court's agenda, a great deal of spadework must be done. At the beginning, the spadework involves giving the subject high visibility in conferences, law school symposia, and articles in national magazines. This book, I suppose, is a good example of the propaganda function in its initial stage. At a later stage, we must work out the details of how law unification should be structured, given the current workload of the federal courts.

When the U.S. Supreme Court decided to unify America's criminal law, the burden thrust on the lower federal courts—which were expected to review state court convictions through habeas corpus proceedings—was substantial. For example, in 1960, before the Supreme Court's precedent-shattering criminal law decisions, postconviction habeas corpus filings in federal district courts amounted to only 1.1. percent of case filings; by 1983, post-conviction habeas corpus filings had risen to 9.5 percent of case filings.[5] Happily for the success of criminal law reform, this net 8.4 percent rearrangement in the federal courts' dockets occurred when the federal courts were expanding their capacity. The appointment of

5. R. Posner, *The Federal Courts: Crisis and Reform* (Cambridge, Mass.: Harvard University Press, 1985), pp. 61–64.

new judges (combined with the reorganization of the courts to allow for the delegation of judicial functions to law clerks and magistrates) allowed this caseload expansion to occur without a significant sacrifice of other activities. It is unlikely, however, that the same could be said for new cases arriving as the result of law unification: it now appears to most observers that there is little excess capacity left in the federal courts.

Practically speaking, therefore, the project of establishing a national common law involves three distinct operations. The first operation consists of endeavors (like this one) designed to explain the need for a national common law. We can call this the propaganda function. The propaganda function involves encouraging serious professional writers (as opposed to academic specialists) to do articles about law unification for magazines like the *Atlantic* and the *New Republic* (both of which are read by judges), and to do shorter pieces for the op-ed pages of major papers like the *New York Times*. In addition, the propaganda function involves seminars at law schools, political science departments, and bar meetings. Perfect forums for discussions of law unification are meetings like the Fourth Circuit Judicial Conference, which convenes every June with at least one U.S. Supreme Court justice and every federal trial and appellate judge in five southeastern states.

The second operation in any overall law unification project can be called the technical function. Initially this involves isolating the areas where the competitive race to the bottom prevails, or where there are conflicting assertions of jurisdiction by competing state courts, both of which would provide us with a specific blueprint of the legal chaos problem in a number of related areas. At that point it should be possible to develop the engineering techniques that can be used to establish a limited and politically acceptable national common law, with due regard to the docket strain on the federal courts. The technical function, unlike the propaganda function, is best performed by academic lawyers who can publish well-thought-out studies in one of the ten major law reviews. Here it is important that articles be published in such places as the *Yale Law and Policy Review,* or the *Harvard Law Review,* rather than in the provincial journals. The law journals with national readerships enjoy a careful peer review that gives them an instant prestige associated only with scholarly authority. In this regard the authority of the law school rubs off on the journal.

Without doubt much of what is written in even the best law

journals approaches *Finnegan's Wake* in practicality and intelligibility. Nonetheless, the truly outstanding articles published in national journals have a significant effect on the contours of the law. Compared with law professors, judges have little time to think or do research. For example, in the 1987 January term of our court, we had over 247 cases on the docket to be decided between January 14 and April 10. That means that roughly 50 cases were assigned to my office for orders or majority opinions. Yet, I was still expected to make some contribution to the other 197 cases. Even allowing for the fact that fully 150 of these cases were simple, routine matters, thinking originally in just the other 47 cases in less than three months would have presented obstacles even to a Nobel laureate. Therefore, judges with novel issues before them repair to the law journals to discover whether some smart professor who has had two full years to think about one narrow problem has figured out a good solution.

A few years ago I was trying to work through the problems of covenants not to compete in employment contracts in a case where every member of our court had a different view of the right answer. In reviewing the journal literature I found a brilliant, twenty-year-old, *Harvard Law Review* article by Professor Harlan M. Blake from the University of Minnesota. The article made sense to me, so I pirated his scheme *in toto*. Furthermore, Professor Blake had thought the problem through so beautifully that when his scheme was reframed as a court opinion it commanded unanimous support among the members of the court.

The third and final operation in the law unification project is implementation. Implementation involves finding cases where the national common law issue can be raised, and then presenting the arguments for national law in a persuasive way in the context of those specific cases. Because courts make law only in actual cases, this is the only way that national law can be achieved. No matter how good a judge may consider an idea, he or she has no vehicle to make a new law until the right case arrives. Yet brilliant theoretical briefs that push out the frontiers of the law may not come easily to the trial lawyers who have the best cases in which to make national law arguments. Just as judges are too overworked to give two years of undivided attention to one complex legal problem, litigating lawyers are overworked and lack the leisure to focus intensively on one narrow problem. Although the great law firms of legal meccas like New York can produce briefs that surpass the

Harvard Law Review in quality, the best cases for presenting national common law arguments may find their way to the Supreme Court from rural Kansas or inner-city Detroit. It is at this point, therefore, that the technical function is of supreme importance; once even overworked litigating lawyers learn that a new way of looking at interstate problems exists, they will use such scholarship as is available to present what they hope will be new, winning arguments.

The implementation function is not limited to arguing cases before the U.S. Supreme Court. Although eventually the Court must endorse the national law concept, other federal and state courts are potentially useful in laying the groundwork for the big Supreme Court ruling. For example, a favorable ruling on the law unification issue from a lower federal appeals court, or even from the highest court of a state, is the quickest imaginable way to force the Supreme Court to put the subject on its agenda. The trick, of course, is to convince a federal circuit court or a state supreme court that the U.S. Supreme Court should be pushed. Pushing that institution requires a lower court decision that presumes to make new law on the grounds that the U.S. Supreme Court would do the same under the facts of the case presented. This, of course, is pure fiction, but it is a polite way of forcing the U.S. Supreme Court to consider an issue that it would otherwise avoid.

Indeed, it would be a rare federal or state court that would be willing to attempt to cudgel the U.S. Supreme Court into a new decision on national law. Yet, unless the national law question is well framed and well argued in the lower court, it will be difficult to get the case into the Supreme Court. The Supreme Court does not usually decide nonjurisdictional issues raised for the first time in that court, so an explicit lower court ruling is needed to frame the issue for appeal.

By now it should be obvious that putting together a program to establish a national common law involves three distinct groups of specialists. First come the propagandists who can explain the problem of legal chaos to broad audiences by discussing such issues as product liability and domestic law. Next come the law professors or foundation staffs who can devote their full energies to working out practical schemes to engineer national common law (something that the propagandists have neither time nor inclination to do). Finally, there are the practicing lawyers who must: (1) be aware of the problem; (2) be informed about the proposed practical solutions; and (3) have real case files on their desks that present opportunities to raise the issue in the context of ongoing lawsuits. Unfortunately, it is unlikely that all of these different groups—motivated as they are by different imperatives—will coordinate their efforts. Therefore, what remains to be found is some coordinating force to bring everyone together.

That force must be business. And business can even find some left-wing allies who might contribute moral support if not money. In fact, I first began to think about the whole uncommon law problem because of domestic cases rather than product liability cases. Although it is of little concern to business, 50 percent of any state trial court's civil docket is taken up with domestic cases: parental kidnapping, interstate flight to avoid paying support, and failure of one state to honor another state's family law decisions are serious, recurring problems. Nonetheless, it would be a complete waste of time for anyone to present the uncommon law problem to the world at large in the context of domestic matters. Nobody with money gives a damn about domestic law. The people who take beatings in family courts can't hire high-priced lawyers or subsidize the presentations of new legal theories. Certainly, domestic litigants are not organized, and to the extent that women victims of poor domestic law have organizations like NOW to speak for them, those organizations run out of money long before they run out of agenda. Domestic law enjoys a low place compared to employment discrimination issues on NOW's agenda anyway.

Business, however, has a surfeit of both money and talent, much of which is currently being squandered on unstructured yelling and screaming about product liability law to Congress and to state legislatures. Business has a much better shot at getting favorable law on product liability from the federal courts than it does from Congress, and, therefore, the courts are where business's resources should go. Business has trade associations and prestigious think tanks like the Heritage Foundation, the American Enterprise Institute, and the Washington Legal Foundation. Here, then, is the organizing force to put together propagandists, legal technicians, and implementers to achieve one narrow, obtainable goal. And, although the average domestic litigant who runs afoul of legal chaos in family courts seldom reads anything more demanding than a Harlequin romance or the *Charleston Gazette*, the national groups that have family law reform as an unfunded item on their agenda are available to provide moral support, some occasional

manpower, and even a little propaganda (particularly if it is written for them).

In *Judicial Jeopardy: When Business Collides with the Courts*,[6] I devoted 200 pages to demonstrating that business currently devotes
roughly 90 percent of its lobbying resources to about 50 percent
of its problems. The 50 percent of business's problems to which it
devotes the lion's share of its resources involves matters before
Congress, state legislatures, executives in power, and administrative agencies. Yet the other 50 percent of business's problems are,
in one way or another, related to the courts. Some court-related
problems, of course, are simply adverse decisions in individual
cases. But other court-related problems proceed from unfavorable
law that is made by judges in their lawmaking capacity. Often this
bad law, which affects business in a general way out-of-court, is
the product of judges' political conclusions arrived at in blissful
ignorance of the problems of the real commercial world.

Because the standard way of discussing law—whether it be official court decisions or commentaries in the law journals—gives
the impression that law is the product of an inaccessible science,
there is a tendency for business to relegate everything involving
the courts to their lawyers. Their lawyers, in turn, become involved in the courts only when they are representing specific
plaintiffs or defendants in pending lawsuits. But, as I have attempted to explain, judges are simply politicians in robes who are
making political decisions based on their best understandings of
society's underlying economic, social, political, and moral imperatives. Obviously, standard lobbying techniques (involving, as they
often do, political contributions and political support) that work
well with legislators and executives are not available when dealing
with judges. But at the heart of all lobbying is supplying decision
makers with honest information. The political contributions and
election support are usually (if not always) simply ways of guaran-
teeing access to busy politicians under favorable conditions (like
a meal or weekend outing). Federal judges don't need campaign
contributions or political support, but that doesn't mean that they
don't need information or high-quality, completed staff work.

Consequently, when I talk about business's coordinating a major
project to get a national common law adopted, what I am really
talking about is a process of lobbying judges. If business lobbyists

6. Addison-Wesley (Reading, Mass.; 1986).

cannot get judges thinking about the problem of our uncommon law over dinner or during a weekend of golf at a high-priced watering hole, sophisticated business lobbyists must get them thinking about it when they read the op-ed page of the *Wall Street Journal* or the *New York Times*. Business lobbyists can also get judges thinking about the problem in *Atlantic Monthly* articles and through the idle chatter of recent law school graduates hired by judges as law clerks. Then, the high quality, completed staff work that emerges in well-written law journal articles can be incorporated in summary form in briefs. The only difference between convincing legislators to do something and convincing judges to do the same thing is that with legislators everything must be explained in terms of the next election, while with judges it must be explained in terms of the next generation.

Chapter 7

Engineering

The biggest mistake that anyone can make when he sets out to improve the courts is to assume that what we need is a bigger and better model of what we already have. This follows from the fact that today's court system is like an old European city whose twentieth-century configuration is dictated by the happenstance of thirteenth-century cow paths, bogs, and streams. The courts of the United States—state and federal—were never intelligently designed at all; they simply evolved from the primitive, *ad hoc* institutions of the early Middle Ages. In the 800-year history of our courts the most prominent phenomenon has been that whenever a problem arose, some *ad hoc,* jury-rigged contraption was added to the system to fix it.

The reason, of course, that courts are only tinkered at, rather than comprehensively redesigned, is that there is little consensus in this society about what it is that we want courts to do. For many customers of the courts' services, the courts provide an unwanted product. Civil courts, after all, are primarily machines for redistributing wealth: when the machinery breaks down, no wealth can be redistributed, and this is obviously an advantage to employers, manufacturers, insurance companies, and anyone else with a deep pocket who is an attractive lawsuit target.

The way courts are organized—in terms of number of judges, delay, appeals procedures, and technical rules—has a decisive effect on the ultimate outcome of lawsuits. The lay-person usually envisages the courts as neutral institutions that resolve legitimate disputes. But, as I have pointed out, the courts are not neutral. The rules are not broadly thought out, and because much of law really

151

reflects the political judgments and emotional passions of the judges, law is only partially a science. Thus, political battles rage in the courts over the same issues that engage the executive and legislative branches. It is rich versus poor, black versus white, male versus female, business versus consumer, developer versus environmentalist, and employer versus workers. Much of the conflict occurs entirely behind the scenes, in areas obscured from public view by the law's inaccessible language and arcane rules. Passionate fights develop over obscure technical matters, such as "standing" to sue a government official, the private causes of action arising from regulatory statutes, and the rules for joining a large number of defendants in a class action suit where the large class is usually on the plaintiffs' side. One way to decide many issues is to overload the courts' meager resources to such an extent that the entire machine breaks down. When that happens, the *status quo* prevails.

In chapter 1, I pointed out that, beginning in the 1960's, there has been a wholesale shift in the center of political power towards the courts and away from legislatures, executives, and administrative agencies. But this shift in the center of power has not gone unnoticed by the actors in the political process outside the court system, or by the community at large. Furthermore, it does not require unusual brilliance to perceive that much of the courts' political strength proceeds from the fact that judges have many of the endearing attributes of military juntas in banana republics. For many constituencies that are frustrated by the slow pace of change and the apparent indifference or corruption of other institutions in the democratic system, the courts offer the possibility of an alternative government—a government independent of elected legislators and executives. The limits to this alternative government, however, are a function of the physical capacity of judges to run things. The most effective judge-control measures, therefore, are simply political techniques that keep judges so busy doing routine criminal cases (the federal *Speedy Trial Act* in criminal cases is a good example), tort suits, and commercial matters that they have no time to become heavily involved in running the government.

The net result of the political battles that rage in the courts, and of the attendant efforts at judge control, is that judges are given logistical support only grudgingly. Any attempt to alter court jurisdiction or tinker at court procedures evokes the type of enthusiasm that would greet a Brahms symphony at a rock concert. Simply put, if you change logistical support, jurisdiction, or court procedure, you also change the mix of winners and losers in the great wealth- and power-distribution game that goes into extra innings every day of the year in every court of the country.

All of this, in turn, has a great bearing on how courts are run, and on all the legal and procedural rules that prevail in court. Yet the most important function that the courts perform is other than deciding the cases that are before them; rather, it lies in the fact that roughly 96 percent of all cases filed in state and federal courts are settled long before trial. But even this figure misses the incalculably larger number of potential lawsuits that are settled after lawyers have been contacted and before papers have been filed in court, or all the potential cases settled by the parties themselves based on what they think the law is. Consequently, the most important function that courts perform is to create a climate hospitable to voluntary settlements.

Although judges are usually reluctant to discuss the settlement function in their formal opinions, much of the way courts are structured centers in their efforts to create an environment conducive to voluntary settlements. If just the criminal cases on any court's docket all went to jury trial instead of being settled by plea bargains, the entire American judicial system would grind to a complete standstill. Thus, a fascinating aspect of the way courts work is the extent to which they are designed around their own structural imperfections or the common failings of humankind.

The greatest challenge in jurisprudence is to reduce as much as possible the extent to which court delay and the complexity of in-court procedures *per se* affect the outcome of lawsuits. Unfortunately, this result is almost never achieved by direct means, such as an expansion of court resources or a wholesale simplification of court procedural rules. Rather, it is accomplished through a carefully crafted balance of terror. At the simplest level, everyone knows that courts are both difficult and expensive to use. Furthermore, because most courts have long waiting lines of litigants seeking jury trials, it is possible for a well-funded defendant to use some combination of complexity and clogged dockets to drag a lawsuit out for years, thus putting a plaintiff and his lawyers to great expense.

The courts, however, have created a counterbalancing terror to dampen this advantage a defendant naturally has: they simply grant juries unbridled discretion to award enormous judgments for pain and suffering, punitive damages, and speculative economic losses. Standing alone, of course, the unbridled discretion given to juries seems utterly absurd; it comes to look sensible only when the long delays and obstructive tactics of defendants are taken into account. When a case actually goes to trial these two countervailing terrors do not necessarily yield a rational result, but they work wonders in the settlement process. All of this, of course, goes on in the background of court processes, while the foreground is dominated by the 4 percent of cases that actually go to trial.

The counterbalancing terrors of court delays and jury awards are easy to understand, but there are more subtle rules that achieve less easily recognized but equally important balances. Of these, perhaps the most important rule involves awards of attorneys' fees. Ostensibly, in the American legal system (as opposed to, say, England's), each litigant is responsible for paying his own attorneys' fees. Thus, plaintiffs will always recover less than they are entitled to, because they must pay for their lawyers, and defendants who successfully beat a lawsuit will still be out their own litigation expenses. Yet, as I have pointed out, the *United States Code* has more than fifty separate fee-shifting statutes that create narrow exceptions to this general rule, and the state legislatures and state courts have created a passel of others. A host of today's legal commentators think that they have invented the jurisprudential equivalent of the wheel, when they suggest that we copy England and institute a "loser pays" rule regarding attorneys' fees.

Indeed, from the point of view of theory, if we think only of the courts' foreground, there is little justification for the American rule. But there is enormous practical justification in the background when we come to understand that the attorneys' fees rule directly relates to conscious decisions about the distribution of wealth and power in American society. The attorneys' fee rule makes little sense standing alone, but in the real world of lawsuits it doesn't stand alone. It is one small part of a comprehensive if imperfect system, and provides balance to other irrational inclinations in that system. For example, in a system where the loser pays both sides' costs, it suddenly becomes practical to hound insolvent debtors ruthlessly, because ultimately the debtor will pay both the cost of the lawsuit *and* the cost of collection. The current rule that each side pays its own lawyers makes it entirely uneconomical to sue either absconding tenants under residential leases, defaulting consumers purchasing on credit, or businesses with which one has a minor commercial dispute.

On the other hand, the same rule—prohibiting, as it does, the shifting of a defendant's cost to a losing plaintiff—enables plaintiffs to sue in personal injury cases and other important matters. If an ordinary worker, injured by a negligently driven Exxon truck, had to weigh the possibility of paying for Exxon's high-priced lawyers if he lost his lawsuit, there would be a strong disincentive to bringing suit. In major lawsuits between poor plaintiffs and rich or insured defendants, a "loser pays" rule would be like offering me a bet where the minimum stake is $100,000, the terms are double or nothing, and the chances of winning are 4 to 1. I can't take advantage of the favorable odds because, in the not entirely unlikely event I lose, I could be wiped out. Furthermore, carried one step further, a "loser pays" rule implies that the middle class with assets will be at an even greater disadvantage than the abjectly poor. At least the abjectly poor could take bankruptcy and lose nothing; the middle class would lose everything. Most people agree with these general, bottom-line results, which is why the attorneys' fee rule is modified only in narrow, specific cases, through limited statutory or decisional law exceptions.

The interesting conclusion that emerges from analysis of the rules governing payment of attorneys' fees is that the frequency and intensity of different types of litigation can be regulated in large measure by tinkering at the rules governing attorneys' fees. For example, in those federal circuits where a majority of the judges are unenthusiastic about class actions, class action suits have been chilled simply through parsimonious calculations by the court of the "reasonable" attorneys' fees payable to the prevailing class action lawyers. The same chilling effect can occur under the federal Civil Rights Act, where the federal statute expressly provides for an award of attorney's fees against the defendant if the plaintiff substantially prevails. But because many civil rights suits ask only for injunctive relief—such as an order that a local jail be brought up to acceptable standards—and not damages, lawyers are reluctant to take them on a contingency basis if the courts pay them only a low hourly fee even if they conclusively win the lawsuit.

Ironically, in today's debate over the proper allocation of power between courts and legislatures, there is a nearly unanimous, tacit acceptance by everyone in the process that legislative solutions to problems are inherently superior to court solutions. Even staunch defenders of judicial activism usually predicate their defense of politically intrusive courts on the theory—advanced here—that legislatures will not act at all and, therefore, court action is better than no action. In fact, however, judicial solutions to social prob-lems that are solved primarily through the courts (in the sense that litigants eventually settle their own disputes in the shadow of the judicial process) are actually superior to legislative solutions. The reason for this result is that judges understand their own court machinery far better than legislators do, and judges can tinker at more court machinery at one time through decisional law than legislators can through specific statutes.

To appreciate the need for a federal, judicial solution to the problem of legal heterogeneity, one need only study attempts to unify national tort law by legislative means. Consider, for example, the *Uniform Contribution Among Tortfeasors Act.* A "tortfeasor" is, of course, one who commits a tort—one whose negligence, reckless-ness, or intentional misconduct causes injury to another. A "joint tortfeasor" is one whose misconduct, along with the misconduct of at least one other person or other legal entity, causes injury to another. "Contribution" is the right of one joint tortfeasor, against whom judgment has been rendered, to recover proportional shares of the judgment from other joint tortfeasors whose miscon-duct contributed to the plaintiff's injury.

Before the Industrial Revolution, most of the torts a person could commit were "intentional" torts—they involved one per-son's injuring another's body, reputation, or property on purpose. In preindustrial times, most tortfeasors were, as the term suggests, wrongdoers. Common law courts denied joint tortfeasors the right of contribution, reasoning that, because they were wrongdoers, they did not deserve the aid of the courts in achieving proportion-ate distribution of judgments rendered against them. The Indus-trial Revolution ushered in all manner of devices that were capa-ble of seriously injuring humans and their property, not out of malice, but simply because they were designed, manufactured, or operated negligently. The appearance of these negligent torts viti-ated the common-law rationale for denying the right of contribu-tion. The law lagged behind technology, however, as it is wont to do, and the common-law rule that one joint tortfeasor could not seek contribution from another remained in force.

The inequity inherent in the common-law denial of the right to contribution was aggravated by the common-law doctrine that an injured plaintiff was "the lord of his action." Suppose, for example, that plaintiff P suffers an injury that is attributable to the negligence of two different companies, A and B. At common law, P could choose to sue both A and B, he could sue one and choose not to sue the other, he could settle with either and sue the other, he could settle with both, or he could just take his lumps and chalk it up to kismet. If P won a judgment against B for the entire amount of his damages, but chose to settle with or not to sue A, B could not recover against A for A's fair share of P's damages, even if A were more at fault than B.

Under this system, the potential for home cooking was enormous. Suppose A manufactures widgets in Ohio, and ships its widgets to B in Pennsylvania, where B puts the gizmos it manufactures together with A's widgets to form a gadget. B then sells a gadget to P, a resident of Ohio. There is a design defect in the widgets manufactured by A. As a result, the gadget B sold to P malfunctions, injuring P. Does P sue A, which pays taxes and provides jobs in his community, donates money to local charities, and whose president is the leader of his son's Boy Scout troop? No! P sues mean, nasty old out-of-state B before a local jury in P's town, and recovers his actual damages and then some. At common law, B was left holding the bag.

By the mid-1930's, the courts and legislatures of several states had either repealed or modified the common-law rule barring contribution among joint tortfeasors. However, of the rules of the various states establishing the right of contribution, no two were the same. In 1936, the American Law Institute and the Conference of Commissioners on Uniform State Laws got together and jointly sponsored the drafting of the *Uniform Contribution Among Tortfeasors Act.* The aim of the ALI and the Commissioners was to draft a uniform statute that would be adopted in all states, thus unifying the national policy on contribution among tortfeasors.

The *Uniform Contribution Among Tortfeasors Act* was unveiled in 1939, amid all of the hip-hooray and ballyhoo that usually attends such watershed events in the history of western civilization. The fanfare was short-lived, however. As of 1955, sixteen years after its initial promulgation, only ten states had adopted the *Uniform Act* in some form or other. Moreover, as the Commissioners themselves noted: "Most of these states have made important changes in the Act which have defeated the whole idea of uniformity; and in anything like its original form it is now in effect only in Arkansas, Hawaii, and South Dakota." Although the right of contribution was by 1955 recognized in nearly half of the states, only the three named commercial meccas had taken the *Uniform Act* seriously. Eight states had statutes that permitted contribution among tortfeasors, but only in cases where the plaintiff had joined the tortfeasor from whom contribution was sought in his original suit. Owing to the "lord of his action" rule, such statutes improved little on the common-law rule. Six other states had broad contribution statutes that merely established the existence of the right of contribution and let the courts work out the details. Six other states had judicially created rules governing contribution.

The Commissioners, unabashed by the failure of their initial effort, set out anew to unify the law in 1955. The result was the new, improved, guaranteed-to-solve-all-of-your-legal-heterogeneity-problems *Uniform Contribution Among Tortfeasors Act of 1955.* For the next ten years the high-powered world of tort reform looked on with awe as all of two states rushed out to enact the 1955 act. The ten jurisdictions that had adopted some form of the 1939 act were so impressed by the 1955 version that they all retained their respective versions of the 1939 effort. Although the 1955 act had by 1986 attracted ten disciples, most of these adopting states made significant changes in the act. Indeed, these ten jurisdictions disagree on fundamental questions, such as whether relative degrees of fault should be considered in determining proportionate shares of contribution among joint tortfeasors.

The heterogeneity built into our national law on contribution by the lack of uniformity in legislation is exacerbated when the courts of the various adopting states interpret their contribution statutes in diverse and idiosyncratic ways. Moreover, 60 percent of our states have elected to adopt neither the 1939 act nor the 1955 act *in any form whatsoever.* Despite the dire need for uniformity in this important area of tort law, scholarly conferences and state legislatures simply cannot get the job done. Ironically, there is now far less uniformity in our national contribution law than there was when every state embraced the simple common-law rule, "if you're sued, you're screwed." And after half a century of huffing, puffing, jawboning, and elbow-rubbing, we are not appreciably closer to a uniform national law on contribution than we were when the ALI and the Commissioners first recognized the need fifty years ago.

None of this is meant to disparage the general competence of legislatures; the bulk of what legislatures do has nothing whatsoever to do with the courts. Perhaps the most important legislative function is the preparation of the budget and the levying of taxes. This process involves the allocation of over a third of our gross national product. Legislatures regulate a host of activities—from interstate communications to the construction of local hospitals—through independent agencies whose day-to-day operations have little to do with the courts.

Often, of course, the help of legislatures is enlisted to reverse unwelcome and perhaps unwholesome decisions already made by the courts. There can be no question that courts and legislatures respond to different constituencies and often have different views of the appropriate social contract. Legislators must be more accommodating than courts to the demands of competing selfish interests. Legislators are largely in the business of pleasing others, while judges, with their life tenure, are largely in the business of pleasing themselves. When, therefore, a result that is terribly satisfying to judges fails to satisfy anyone else, outraged constituents repair to the legislature for help. Usually, help is not forthcoming, but the theoretical possibility of help provides a healthy safety valve for pent-up outrage and provides the illusion of democratic redress. Much of the time, however, courts and legislatures move in the same direction; when this occurs, judicial solutions are often superior to legislative solutions if it is the courts that must ultimately apply the solution to the problem. And, as the example concerning the *Uniform Contributions Among Tortfeasors Act* clearly demonstrates, a federal court solution to problems of heterogeneity is far superior to a legislative solution that requires coordinated efforts among all fifty states.

When we are dealing with problems that relate directly to the courts, another reason that court-designed solutions may be better than legislative solutions is that legislatures take seriously what the courts say about themselves. Court opinions mainly focus on what happens in court, and these opinions tend to wax eloquent about the precision of the in-court, truth-finding function. But judges understand that much of what they say about the sanctity of juries or the allocation of negligence among different defendants is written tongue-in-cheek. What is really important in regulating society through the courts happens out of court. Things like the rules of evidence, or the extent of pre-trial discovery, are insignificant in comparison to rules governing attorneys' fees, or the balance of terror between long docket delays and monstrous jury awards. When plaintiffs' lawyers will take cases for contingency fees and there is no penalty for losing a suit, lots of cases get filed in court that are ultimately settled out-of-court. But place the burden of a winning defendant's attorneys' fees on the losing plaintiff, and overnight the entire mix of lawsuits changes.[1]

Legislators, like everyone else, are expected to take what courts say about themselves with a straight face. Congress could hardly pass a law whose underlying supposition is that *Erie Railroad v. Tompkins* was simply a result-oriented, *ad hoc,* populist decision of a New Deal court. No matter how silly Congress may believe *Erie* to be, it would at least need to pretend to take seriously its supposedly eternal verities about federalism, and couch any statute overruling the *Erie* result in language paying lip service to the *Erie* reasoning. Courts may know deep in their guts that much of what they write is nonsense, but the system breaks down if others don't at least pretend to take them seriously. Consequently, when Con-

---

1. There is a similarity here to a phenomenon that occurs in literature: some writers, like Homer, place everything in the foreground where it can immediately be grasped by the reader. Other writers, like the authors of the Bible, however, assume that the reader shares a common background with the writer, so that much of importance to the story occurs in the background. See E. Auerbach, *Mimesis: The Representation of Reality in Western Literature* (Princeton: Princeton University Press, 1953). Legislators tend to deal in a world where everything of importance occurs in the foreground, while judges and lawyers deal in a world where most things of importance occur in the background. For example, court review of administrative agency decisions is really about the quality of the decision maker who will decide issues crucial to our lives. Administrative agencies are highly susceptible to political pressure and have a natural tendency to expand their turf. Furthermore, the people in the agency are often hotshot kids with great paper credentials but little practical experience. Federal and state judges, on the other hand, usually have no political ax to grind, and they are gray-haired and experienced in life. Yet you will never find a reversal of an administrative agency decision explicitly based on the agency's politics or its staff's inexperience. When reversing administrative agencies, courts always talk about the agency's failure to consider certain evidence, or about some ostensible defect in the notice or hearing apparatus. Skilled lawyers know that they can get an administrative ruling overturned simply by showing a court that the ruling is stupid, notwithstanding the perfection of the procedures used to reach the decision at the agency level. All of this, however, is obscure background and can't be figured out from published opinions. It is like the New Testament's casual reference to Jesus' descent from the House of David; without a knowledge of the Prophecies of the Old Testament, the importance of Jesus' lineage makes no sense.

gress or a state legislature passes a law designed to reform some apparent abuse in the judicial process, the legislators must accept every other aspect of the judicial process as given. The result of taking everything else in the existing judicial system as a given is a spectacularly complicated statute with wildly convoluted procedures that do little to remedy the malady the legislature set out to cure.

Examples of this phenomenon are the 1986 Senate version of the product liability reform bill (SB 2760), and the 1986 statute limiting the liability of vaccine manufacturers. Both of these bills are more complicated than Aquinas's justification for the existence of God. And a comparison of the vaccine bill (that actually passed both Houses of Congress) with the product liability bill that didn't come close to passing, demonstrates that it is almost impossible for Congress to intrude successfully into a highly political, court-dominated, wealth-redistribution program.

After establishing a complicated but largely useless settlement mechanism, SB 2760 (the product liability bill) goes on to limit manufacturers' liability for defective products both in terms of damages recoverable and the grounds for suit. Among other features of SB 2760, distributors of products are not liable to suit if the manufacturer can be sued; noneconomic losses are limited to $250,000; and manufacturers' liability for punitive damages is severely restricted. The Senate definitely wants to reform product liability law, but even in the Senate version of the bill there is so much weasel language and so many exceptions to the general scheme that the bill is likely to have little effect on the average products lawsuit. Furthermore, all of this fudging has happened in the Senate, *before* the bill goes to the hostile House, where it can be expected either to be killed entirely or so thoroughly gutted that it will no longer be acceptable to its original sponsors.

It is hard to summarize SB 2760 without setting forth the whole bill, but one section may demonstrate how legislatures take court processes more seriously than the courts would themselves. Section 303(a) of SB 2760 provided:

> Punitive damages may, if otherwise permitted by applicable law, be
> awarded in any civil action subject to this title to any claimant
> who establishes by clear and convincing evidence that the harm
> suffered was the result of conduct manifesting a manufacturer's
> or product seller's conscious, flagrant indifference to the safety
> of those persons who might be harmed by a product. A failure

to exercise reasonable care in choosing among alternative
product designs, formulations, instructions or warnings is not of
itself such conduct. Except as provided in subsection (b) of this
section, punitive damages may not be awarded in the absence of
a compensatory award.

The Senate bill says all of this with a straight face; there is no
apparent recognition that juries aren't concerned with the difference between "clear and convincing evidence" and the normal
"preponderance of the evidence" standard for recovery. Judges,
however, know that when juries want to help injured victims they
don't care about the weight of the evidence. The "clear and convincing" standard does allow both the original trial court and a
reviewing appellate court to set a jury verdict aside as contrary
to the evidence, but that requires judges who actively seek pro-
defendant results.

The truth of the matter, of course, is that a pro-defendant judge
can set jury verdicts aside now if he or she wants, and it happens
all the time with regard to the amount of judgments. In the course
of the last fifteen years the personnel on our own court has
changed four times, which means that I have actually served on
four separate courts. So far, however, I haven't seen one that was
pro-defendant. All skilled lawyers for plaintiffs know how to characterize the facts in a case so as to get the punitive damages question to the jury, and the jury in turn does its usual number on the
defendant. Furthermore, my bet is that the first place the House
of Representatives will start its bill-gutting process will be the
"clear and convincing evidence" standard. If a bill like SB 2760
ever passes, the House will manage to delete the "clear and convincing evidence" standard.

The vaccine bill that Congress passed in 1986 set up an admit-
tedly useful no-fault scheme for handling weak claims against vaccine manufacturers when the plaintiff happens to be the one inoc-
ulee in a million who has a serious reaction to a standard vaccine.
However, the strong claims—where the plaintiff is likely to win a
big award from a jury—are expressly exempted from the operation of the bill, which leaves most of the problems that the bill was
supposed to solve exactly where they were before the bill's passage.

The reason, therefore, why I say court solutions to court-related
problems are better is that, when the courts decide to make a major policy change, they know enough about their own system to
enable them to restructure all of the counterbalancing terrors at

the same time. In other words, the courts are able to rearrange both the foreground *and* the background, while a legislature is likely to tinker exclusively at the foreground. The best example of this is the Supreme Court's radical realignment in the law of libel in *New York Times v. Sullivan.* Not only did the Supreme Court provide definite, bright-line guidance concerning what did or did not constitute actionable libel by a media defendant, the Supreme Court also eliminated any local jury fudge factor.

In *New York Times,* the Supreme Court simply said that in libel cases the trial judge is the ultimate arbiter of both the law and the facts. That means that regardless of applicable state law, in all libel cases a trial court judge must expressly agree with the jury's verdict, and all reviewing appellate courts must also make independent evaluations of the evidence. This simple rule demonstrates a complete mastery of the "background" in the judicial process, because it precludes a state court from falling back on the old rule that a jury's verdict will not be disturbed unless it is clearly contrary to the weight of the evidence. The Supreme Court understands that plaintiffs win before juries, and that most juries either don't understand the court's instructions or don't take those instructions seriously. But under *New York Times,* a reviewing state court must write an opinion showing how the plaintiff proved that the defendant published false information that the defendant either knew or should have known to be false, and that it did so with the specific intent to injure the plaintiff. With that firm rule governing media libel, it is hardly surprising that plaintiffs have had a notably unspectacular track record since *New York Times.* The Supreme Court set out to protect robust free discussion in the press and succeeded more or less completely. We can quarrel with the court's wisdom but not with its craftsmanship. Unlike SB 2760, there has been little weasel language in the First Amendment cases of the last twenty-five years.

Unless we can say that one of the law's desirable goals is full employment for lawyers, the best legal rules are characterized by supreme simplicity rather than monstrous complexity. A bill like SB 2760 is monstrously complex. For example, if the Supreme Court wanted to take control of state product liability law because of the competitive race to the bottom, the Court could do most of what SB 2760 attempts to do with one simple rule. That rule would be that in product liability cases an offer of a fair settlement to the plaintiff within ninety days of notice of the claim insulates the manufacturer from punitive damages, unless it can be shown that the manufacturer actually knew that the product was unreasonably dangerous and deliberately sold it in the face of such knowledge. And, if the Supreme Court wants to eliminate all of the fudge in such a rule, it can repair to the *New York Times* technique of making the trial court judge the final arbiter of the facts as well as of the law. Under such a rule there would be a presumption against punitive damages in all cases, and the punitive damages issue could go to a jury in the face of a fair settlement offer only upon the judge's explicit determination in the first instance that there was clear and convincing evidence to support such an award. Furthermore, what constitutes a "fair" settlement offer should be a matter for the trial court judge: to be "fair" a settlement offer need not be as much as a jury ultimately gives, but it must be in keeping with what knowledgeable lawyers would agree to voluntarily on behalf of their clients in similar cases. It is because of the opportunity for rules like this, as I said earlier, that it is possible for the courts to make both plaintiffs and defendants better off at the same time. The only losers would be highly paid lawyers who would have little to litigate about.

When courts and legislatures set out to craft legal rules, one of their greatest problems is that they attempt to do perfect justice.[2] But in attempting to do *perfect* justice the rules often become so complicated that all the bright lines disappear, which then leaves us in a position worse than that in which we would be with rougher but more easily understood rules. In applying my suggested rule about punitive damages, some very careless and malevolent manufacturers will undoubtedly get off lightly; but the tradeoff is that almost everyone who is seriously injured by a product will get *paid* within ninety days. There is still a hole for the real evildoers, but the ordinary incompetent manufacturer will not be terrorized, and the ordinary victim will see some quick money. Furthermore, this rule makes explicit something that is going on anyway: Punitive damages are mostly used as a lever to force settlements favorable to the plaintiff.

There are a few other product liability problems that also need to be settled by bright-line rules. One involves what happens when someone uses a product beyond its useful life, and another con-

---

2. See in this regard, but in the context of the criminal law, M. Fleming, *The Price of Perfect Justice* (New York: Basic Books, 1974).

cerns a manufacturer's liability for products like drugs or aircraft that have been approved by an appropriate regulatory agency. These issues are generally handled well in SB 2760, but there are still loopholes and weasel language that might be avoided in a strong court opinion. It is particularly in these areas that we see state law today shaped by the typical profile of a product suit—in-state plaintiff, in-state jury, in-state court, and out-of-state defendant. The law on these two subjects in most American jurisdictions now seems to be that the deep pocket pays regardless—even if the consumer opens a can of gasoline with a blowtorch.

The monumental difficulty we have passing any statute on law unification points out a further problem with statutes that can be avoided by using federal decisional law. Not only are law unification statutes like SB 2760 hard to pass in the first instance, they are nearly impossible to amend once they have been passed. A headline in the *Wall Street Journal* on 23 May 1986 read: "Effort to Change Liability Law Is Joined By Labor, Business, Professional Groups." The lead paragraph said: "Organized labor and an extensive, new coalition of professional and business groups joined those calling for changes in liability laws at both the state and federal level." This report implies a greater level of cooperation and unity of purpose among traditionally opposing forces than is common in business-related matters, which may account for SB 2760's passage in the Senate. However, if a similar bill passes both Houses of Congress in any form, it is eminently unlikely that another strong, uncommon alliance will materialize to amend the original scheme as problems develop in its application. Decisional law, on the other hand, can be changed constantly at the margin to improve and refine the original concept.

The decisional law development process that occurs constantly at the margin can be seen today in one of the U.S. Supreme Court's major law-unification projects—criminal procedure. Over the last four years many of the severe restrictions on police conduct that emerged during the first decade of "constitutionalizing" state criminal law have been relaxed in the face of overwhelming evidence that those restrictions have little or no effect on enhancing civil liberties or deterring police misconduct. For example, up until 1984, if a defendant were arrested or his house searched under a defective warrant, any evidence against him obtained through the arrest or search under the defective warrant was excluded from trial. But in 1984 the Supreme Court modified the exclusionary rule to allow an exception if the police, in good faith, believe that they have a good warrant when they make an arrest or search. In changing the decisional law in this regard the Supreme Court pointed out that defective warrants are usually the result of technical errors by low-level magistrates and not errors on the part of the police. Continuing the more severe rule, the Supreme Court said, was unlikely to improve judicial competence in minor courts but would confound justice by freeing the guilty. The Court explicitly found that there was no desirable policy to be served by placing the onus of judicial errors on the police, who have a right to rely on the judges.

In a similar vein, in 1986 the Supreme Court changed its rule that the police could not continue to interrogate a defendant after he asked for a lawyer. The old rule was very strict—once a person asked for a lawyer, all interrogation had to cease even though the defendant might express a willingness to continue talking. Under the strict old rule many voluntary confessions were excluded from evidence on the basis of this procedural technicality, even though the excluded confessions were the best available evidence of guilt. Under the new holding, however, the mere fact that the defendant expresses a desire for a lawyer does not *ipso facto* preclude further police interrogation if the defendant initiates the discussion and knowingly waives his right to remain silent.

Neither of these changes has met with acclaim among civil libertarians, but most participants in the criminal-law process believe that both these modifications are appropriate corrections that will have no negative effect on civil liberties and will avoid some outrageous miscarriages of justice. Yet if a national system of criminal procedure had been accomplished by federal statute rather than constitutional interpretation, it is unlikely that technical amendments tinkering at the margin of criminal procedure in this way would pass Congress very often. (Of course, as we all know, no general criminal-procedure statute enhancing civil liberties would ever have passed in the first place, because of the resistance of the die-hard-law-and-order lobby.)

The history of national criminal procedure instructs our understanding of the whole subject of fashioning national law, because it points out how little we actually know about the real world when we start making social policy. We think that we know certain things, and indeed, we may actually know what we think we know, but as time goes on the solution to the problem changes the problem. The U.S. Supreme Court's expansion of civil liberties through a national law of criminal procedure began in earnest in the middle sixties with cases like *Gideon v. Wainright* and *Miranda v. Arizona. Gideon* involved an indigent criminal defendant's right to court-appointed counsel in all serious cases, and *Miranda* involved a defendant's right to remain silent during police interrogation. The theory on which the new criminal procedure was grounded was that by releasing guilty felons when the police failed to honor civil liberties, the engines of criminal justice would improve their performance. And that is largely what happened: police departments began extensive training programs and instructed their officers to do everything by the book; state governments devised schemes to assure every defendant a competent, court-appointed lawyer at state expense; lay justices of the peace were either replaced by lawyer magistrates, or upgraded through extensive training programs; and, the police were forced to rely on sound investigations rather than on coerced confessions. In short, there was wholesale institutional reform in the rats' nests that were local police stations and county courthouses. By 1975 we could be proud that the indigent young stranger who ran afoul of the criminal law while traveling through a small town was no longer treated simply as meat on the way to dressing and processing.

But by the middle 1980's it became obvious to everyone that there were limits to this upgrading process. In fact, in 1977, our own state court ran afoul of these inherent limits and did something that in retrospect was very silly. Since I wrote the majority opinion, the lion's share of the blame is mine. Simply put, we attempted to duplicate at the state level some of the Supreme Court's achievement at the national level in the area of institutional reform. Waterloo arrived, however, when we set out to improve our state's method of handling troubled juveniles.[3] In 1977

---

3. In 1942, when my grandfather was governor, he once became so outraged over the way the Industrial School for Boys (i.e., the reform school) was operated that he made a surprise visit and fired the superintendent on the spot. He also physically assaulted one of the guards and then fired him because he was carrying a stick with a belt nailed to its end for use in beating the inmates. He then threatened to fire every employee at the school if conditions didn't improve. They may have improved marginally for awhile, but in 1973, when I made my first inspection of the boy's reformatory as a judge, all of its inmates looked to me like Millet's "Man with a Hoe." It seemed to me that there was little light behind the inmates' eyes, and this I attributed to bad management and a terrible staff.

we had two industrial schools, one each for boys and girls, to which both criminal offenders and disturbed children were sent. The disturbed children are technically called "status offenders," because they are guilty of such juvenile offenses as running away, ungovernability, or promiscuous sexual liaisons that would not be punishable if they were adults. Thus their violations of the penal code are entirely related to their "status" as children.

In the case of *Harris v. Calendine,* in a decision which I wrote for the court, we held that status offenders can never be housed in the same facility with criminal offenders. Our purpose in making such a holding was simply to force the state legislature to provide modern therapeutic facilities for children with serious emotional or family problems. If left without help, the relatively benign status offender will almost certainly become a criminal offender in about two weeks on the street, and this result is unlikely to be avoided simply by shipping the status offender off to reform school for an eleven-month sojourn with juvenile armed robbers, rapists, murderers, and arsonists. But the reaction that our court expected from the legislature never occurred; instead of the legislature's passing a statute establishing a good school for the residential treatment of troubled children, the legislature basically said, "The hell with it!" The result was that for many years runaways and ungovernable teenagers simply ran wild in the streets; the situation got so bad that children actually carried around xeroxed copies of the court's opinion in *Harris v. Calendine* to show the police when they were threatened with arrest. The kids themselves were quick to point out that they could not be arrested and detained, because the state had no facilities that qualified under the *Harris* opinion to receive them. Furthermore, fearful of civil rights suits, the police departments threw up their hands and stopped arresting street kids, truants, and runaways.

But if the court had known in advance how little legislative interest there would be in juvenile problems, we would have crafted the court's ruling differently. Among other things, we would probably have permitted the same facility to be used for both criminal and status offenders if it were appropriately divided and each group segregated from the other. What we did not understand at the time we decided *Harris* was that the deterrence value of a traditional reform school for children who were truant or ungovernable was extremely significant at the grass roots level. Without the credible threat of a truly miserable place for repeat status offenders, the alternatives of probation and group homes run by private charities lost their attractiveness. Once children understood that we had no place to send them that complied with *Harris v. Calendine,* they thumbed their noses at the whole system.[4] Unfortunately we had focused our attention on the part of the system we could see—namely, the miserable place to which status offenders had to be sent if secure detention was required. But we did not understand entirely the part of the system that we could not see—namely, all the cases successfully handled at the local level with a slap on the wrist, probation, or commitment to a private, non-secure group home.

On a nationwide basis we have had other, similar experiences. For example, during the 1970's the courts took the lead in forcing the deinstitutionalization of mental patients. The community placement movement for the mentally ill arose from the Dickensian squalor of the state mental hospitals, and the fact that many patients who could live higher-quality lives were kept like animals in those hospitals simply through lack of medical resources or bureaucratic incompetence. But the result of deinstitutionalization has been a dramatic increase in our "homeless" population, as former mental patients have been released with little or no continuing support. Again, the assumptions that courts made about how legislatures would respond to rulings requiring humane treatment for the mentally ill were completely confounded.

Thus the lesson to be learned from our experience in the last twenty years at both federal and state levels is that information about how society actually works is slow in coming. When a change is made through an intricately detailed statute, there is a high likelihood that one imperfect solution to a problem today will be carved in stone forever, with little latitude to adjust as the solution changes the problem. Both the decisional law and the broad, general statutes that leave much room for court rearrangement of the specifics are infinitely superior to statutes like SB 2760 with all their galloping complexity. Probably the best product liability bill imaginable would simply be a short authorization for the federal courts to establish a national law of product liability.

---

4. It was, indeed, remarkable to me how quickly the juvenile subculture picked up on our court's ruling. Although children may be generally ignorant of current events, they apparently have a lightning-fast intelligence system about public issues that directly affect their own personal lives.

If I were drafting a short statute authorizing federal courts to nationalize product liability law, I would initially place *supervisory* jurisdiction over the subject in federal courts (although cases would still be tried in state courts) and then go on to direct the federal courts to craft the law, taking into consideration the following: (1) employment opportunities; (2) insurance availability and cost; (3) the ability of manufacturers to insure for risks unknown to them at the time of product manufacture; (4) the desirability of quick settlement of all meritorious claims; (5) the proper allocation of attorneys' fees; (6) the desirability of encouraging the manufacture of safe products; and, (7) justice to persons injured by defective products, and the desirability of spreading inevitable individual risks among society as a whole.

In the statute's preamble I would distill the analysis in chapter 3 concerning the competitive race to the bottom, to provide a commerce clause justification for federal jurisdiction. This, in fact, is the general outline of numerous successful federal statutes. The outstanding example of the technique may be our antitrust law which has been developed under the authority of the comparatively short and general *Sherman* and *Clayton* acts. Neither of these statutes comes close to the detail of SB 2760, and yet a comprehensive body of decisional law has been constructed under their authority. In fact, even though antitrust is ostensibly governed by federal statutes, the antitrust laws are an example of a constantly changing, flexible body of doctrine that looks more like common law than like rigid statutory law.

Ever since the passage of the *Sherman Act* in 1896 the courts have tinkered at appropriate definitions of "monopoly," "attempt to monopolize," "conspiracy," and "line of commerce." These concepts have changed as the nature of American industry has changed, taking into consideration such factors as foreign competition, economies of scale, barriers to entry, and concentrations of political power. Antitrust specialists have been dissatisfied with the antitrust law for more than eighty years, but their dissatisfaction is related more to the specific results that they want to achieve than it is to the law's technical imperfections. Proponents of big business want the law to be more sensitive to economies of scale and to learning curve phenomena—in other words "big" should not be synonymous with "bad"—while the liberals want tighter control of bigness *per se.* The courts have not done a perfect job of sorting out the antitrust mess, but they have certainly done a better job than Congress could have done by establishing every criterion of the law through a hundred-page statute resistant to amendment.

But all considerations of technical engineering aside for a moment, there is a political advantage in advocating the type of broad, open-ended statute that I suggest. Such a statute has a higher likelihood than available alternatives like SB 2760 of actually passing. Based on my own legislative experience, a reincarnated SB 2760 is unlikely to pass any session of Congress, and if it should ever be so modified as to be acceptable to the House, it will be so defanged as to be less than useless. A general statute, on the other hand, has the political advantage of postponing to another day the gruesome details of whose ox will ultimately be gored, and (happily for Congress) the ox-goring function will be performed by the courts while congressmen yell "dirty sons of bitches" at the judges. Certainly the criteria that I have enumerated are largely unobjectionable: who, for example, is *against* employment or insurance availability? Manufacturers, on the other hand, cannot voice public objections to the desirability of safe products or of spreading the risk of unavoidable accidents. The plaintiff's bar has a high regard for the quality of federal decisional law, and the manufacturers are bound to get a better shake under any national law scheme than they are currently getting under parochial state law.

There is, of course, a major mechanical obstacle to the general statute I propose. Under SB 2760 and any other comprehensive product liability statute, the law applies directly in state courts as well as federal courts. Since most product liability suits are brought in state court and cannot be removed to federal court, the statute must direct both state and federal courts to craft the product liability law according to the criteria of the statute. Decisions of the highest courts of states, then, would be appealable to the Supreme Court of the United States. The difference, however, between that system and the one we currently have is that now, under *Erie v. Tompkins,* the various federal trial courts must follow the decisional law of the states in which they sit. Under my broad federal statute, however, the state courts would be required to follow federal precedent. Ultimately the result would be uniformity, but there would be a race to see whether a federal or state case reached the U.S. Supreme Court first.

Such a broad general statute gives everyone in the process an opportunity to gather, in an organized way, a lot of information that will instruct us in figuring out what the new court-made law should look like. For example, we don't really know what effect product liability law has on employment. There is anecdotal evidence that some manufacturers have been put out of business by product suits, and we understand the special problem of asbestos litigation. But how pervasive is the employment effect? We don't really know for sure. Furthermore, we also don't know the exact extent to which liability law rather than insurance company misjudgment has been responsible for the so called "insurance crisis." According to Jury Verdict Research, a firm in Solon, Ohio, that gathers data on court phenomena, the average jury award in product liability cases between 1975 and 1984 rose only slightly faster than inflation.

There is also significant evidence that the unavailability of liability insurance is related more to the rapidly declining rate of interest in the 1980's than it is to any expansion of liability or increase in jury awards. During the late seventies and early eighties, when interest rates approached 18 percent, insurance companies actively solicited risky business because the high earnings on reserves more than compensated for high-risk coverage. When interest rates fell, however, losses exceeded net earnings for several years, causing general panic throughout the industry.

In this last regard, Edward J. Noha, Chairman and Chief Executive Officer of CNA Insurance Companies, made the following observation during a meeting of the National Association of Insurance Commissioners on June 11, 1985:

> [L]et me also emphasize that today's problems of availability and affordability cannot all be laid at the door of the civil justice system. There is ample blame to go around. Insurers have made a number of mistakes, particularly in the ways they've responded to the high competitive environment of the last few years. This includes the direct insurers, of course—but it's also true that the availability of cheap reinsurance greatly exacerbated the problem. And so did the widespread actions of agents who sold their products as commodities on price alone and underplayed their roles as responsible risk managers. . . . Yet as true as this is, the hard reality is that a massive share of the blame must be shouldered by the civil justice system and its apparent antagonism toward the traditional insurance mechanism. . . .

[L]ast year's $4 billion operating loss—a loss after investment income—has finally put to bed the popular image of an industry crying over underwriting unprofitability all the way to the bank.

Although a general statute on product liability has a better chance of passage than a specific statute like SB 2760, it's still very much an uphill fight. Nonetheless, proposing and lobbying for a general statute has some educational side effects that are valuable in and of themselves. As it currently stands, the problems of product liability are usually discussed in terms of the law's ultimate effect on the distribution of wealth: that makes it easy for injured victims to make an attractive case against greedy manufacturers. So far, however, no one has focused on the inherent parochial bias of the process that makes product liability law. If, therefore, the center of attention is changed from specific results in particular circumstances (the liability, for example, of manufacturers of products approved by a federal regulatory agency) to the inequity of the process by which the law is made, perhaps broader support for reform can be enlisted. Even if one firmly believes, as I do, that ultimately our relief from the uncommon law will come through the Supreme Court of the United States and not from anything Congress does, banging the uncommon law problem home on Capitol Hill for a few years must inevitably be helpful as part of the overall propaganda offensive.

I have devoted much of what I have said to such problems as interstate family matters, conflicts of law, competitive but inconsistent state court rulings in tax matters, and product liability—problems that need to be fixed because the machinery is broken. But in the grand scheme of a national common law there are upside possibilities that are related more to new flights of imagination than they are to solving specific, existing problems. One such opportunity springs from the fertile mind of Professor Robert B. Reich of the Kennedy School of Government at Harvard.[5] According to Professor Reich, successful entrepreneurship requires significant investment by both management and workers in one another. These mutual investments defy boxing in using the techniques of traditional contract law, and, therefore, must be based on mutual trust. For example, if a manufacturer decides to build

5. The most comprehensive presentation of Professor Reich's ideas appear in *Tales of a New America* (New York: Random House, Times Books, 1987).

a component himself rather than to buy it from Japan, he must invest money in training his workers to perform the new function. Once trained, however, the workers become more valuable to other employers and may demand a wage hike that destroys the original advantage the American manufacturer had in producing the product himself rather than buying it from abroad. As it currently stands, neither traditional contract law nor traditional labor law provides an escape from a dilemma such as this.

In order for management to be willing to take risks to expand employment, or for workers to stay with a company that trained them even when the company's profits and wages are down, there must be mutual trust and a joint commitment to the success of the firm. Unfortunately, today's contract law actually discourages such mutual trust by encouraging everything to be set forth in black and white, while refusing to enforce many of the "hidden handshakes." In a commercial world where the law has little use for reliance in any "trust" that can't be reduced to printed clauses in a written agreement, there will always be attractive opportunities to profit from perfidy and trust-breaking. Obviously, managers who feel exploited by departing employees are less generous to subsequent employees, and workers who have been mistreated by management once are reluctant to be suckers again.

As Professor Reich puts it:

> ... [R]ed tape multiplies in parallel with the profusion of finagles it seeks to contain, and vice versa. As contractual refinements progress, litigation over them also escalates, for each party feels compelled to contest adverse interpretations of the ever more convoluted contracts and rules. Employees sue managers, shareholders sue directors, creditors sue those who audited the corporate books, everyone sues the companies that insure everyone against liability.
>
> Those who get paid for rearranging economic assets, rather than enhancing their value, have a not inconsiderable pecuniary interest in the continued deterioration of commercial trust. The business pages of the morning paper offer continuous news of novel ploys and counter-ploys of paper entreprenuers seeking to outmaneuver one another. Every new thrust invites a more sophisticated parry, requiring an ever larger number of lawyers, accountants, and financial advisers to execute it."[6]

6. R. B. Reich, "Enterprise and Double Cross," *Washington Monthly,* January 1987, p. 18.

The perverse dynamics that Professor Reich describes are difficult to unravel (if for no other reason than that "trust" obligations are more easily enforced against management than against workers), but most of us have experienced the need for trust in our business relations. That, indeed, is why we prefer to do business with our friends. Most of us see Professor Reich's dynamics at work every day, and grope for ways to mitigate their pernicious effects. To the extent that new legal doctrines must be developed in the next twenty years in furtherance of a national industrial policy that encourages management and workers to cooperate, rather than view one another as adversaries, those doctrines must be developed at the national level.

Finally, it is probably important to admit that much of what I have written here is written with some reluctance. There is a vitality, accessibility, and accountability in the American federal system that I find missing in countries like England and France with their centralized system of management. Obviously, we have been chipping away at federalism for two hundred yars, and one wonders whether this constant chipping will ultimately leave nothing at all. But the role I envisage for the federal courts in the process of law unification is reasonably small, given the breadth of American law. And the limited reserve of federal court resources dictates that the day-to-day administration of national law must still largely proceed in state courts. In fact, we can reasonably expect that, with their crowded dockets, the federal courts won't be out looking for any more work than it is absolutely necessary for them to perform.

If, however, I appear to be less than appropriately sensitive to federalism principles, it is simply because I am old enough to have lived in the shadow of the depression and to understand the political implications that economic catastrophe holds for a free society. Current double-digit unemployment rates in Europe and the 1987 collapse of our stock market lead me to believe that a replay of the 1930's is not beyond possibility. Part of avoiding a serious economic calamity is the delicate balancing of the requirements of economic growth against considerations of environmental and social justice. Ultimately, to be successful, we must make decisions as a unified, forward-thinking nation, and not as a hodgepodge of uncoordinated, independent states. Thus, to that end I am willing to sacrifice a little federalism. I still believe with Hamilton that the courts are the least dangerous branch of government.

Index